Islam in a Globalizing World

THOMAS W. SIMONS, JR.

Stanford Law and Politics
An imprint of Stanford University Press
Stanford, California 2003

To the memory of
Sir Hamilton A. R. Gibb
(1895–1971)

Stanford University Press
Stanford, California

The Institute for International Studies at Stanford University
has graciously provided funds in support of this publication.

Printed in the United States of America
on acid-free, archival-quality paper

Library of Congress Cataloging-in-Publication Data

Simons, Thomas W, Jr.
Islam in a globalizing world / Thomas W. Simons, Jr.
    p.   cm.
Includes bibliographical references and index.
ISBN 0-8047-4811-x (cloth : alk. paper)—
ISBN 0-8047-4833-0 (pbk. : alk. paper)
1. Islam—History. 2. Islam and politics—History.
3. Islamic fundamentalism—History. 4. Islam—21st century.
5. Globalization—Religious aspects—Islam.
                                        I. Title.
BP50.S56 2003
297'.09—DC21
2003000526

Original Printing 2003

Last figure below indicates year of this printing:
12   11   10   09   08   07   06   05   04   03

Typeset by Tim Roberts in 11/14 Garamond

Contents

This book by Ambassador Thomas W. Simons, Jr., explores the development of Islam in the context of a changing world, an issue that has become the focus of enormous and worldwide public interest. It is a tragedy that it took the events of September 11, 2001, to bring home to us in the United States how poorly we understand Islam.

Tom Simons has written this book on the basis of the Payne Memorial Lectures *Islam in a Globalizing World*, which he gave at the Institute for International Studies at Stanford University in the winter quarter of 2002. It is an important contribution to expanding our knowledge and understanding of Islam.

The Payne Lectures were established to provide people with experience in international affairs an opportunity to address the great international issues of our day. Tom Simons's distinguished career in diplomacy, including a term as United States ambassador to Pakistan, equipped him well to give these lectures.

We are grateful to Ambassador Simons for these lectures, and to members of the Payne family for making the lecture series possible.

David Holloway
Director, Institute for International Studies
Stanford University

Acknowledgments

This book began as the Arthur and Frank Payne Distinguished Lectures for the academic year 2001–2, at Stanford University. Delivered in February and March 2002, the lectures bore the same title as the present book. The Payne lectureship is one of America's finest vehicles for thinking and commentary on public affairs in general and on international relations in particular. I owe the Payne family a debt of gratitude for establishing it.

I am also grateful to the Stanford scholars who brought me to one of the world's great academic communities upon my retirement from thirty-five years in the U.S. Foreign Service, who supported me there for three wonderful years, and who brought me back for the Payne Lectureship. Thanks to Norman M. Naimark, a friend for decades, I was Consulting Professor of 20th-Century International History from 1998 to 2002. Some of this essay began in my History Department colloquia on "Great Ideological Movements of the 20th Century: Socialism and the Islamic Revival" (1998–99), "20th-Century Turkey, Iran, and Pakistan" (1999–2000), and

"Varieties of Islamic Revival Since 1870" (2000–2001). Thanks to Scott D. Sagan, I was (and remain) Consulting Professor at the Center for International Security and Cooperation (CISAC), of which he is codirector. And it is thanks to the leadership of the Institute for International Studies, which sponsors the Payne Lectureship, that this opportunity came my way. I am therefore especially grateful to its director, David J. Holloway, and its deputy director, Coit D. Blacker, a fellow veteran of some of Washington's bureaucratic wars in the early 1990s.

These reflections have also been shaped by large chunks of personal and professional experience before Stanford. In my case, these two aspects of life are intertwined, since I was raised in a family that joined U.S. diplomacy in 1945, when I was seven. My debt of gratitude to my parents, Thomas W. and Mary Jo Simons, is very deep. It was they who took me in 1945 to a British India festering with Hindu-Muslim tension, and then, three years later, to newly independent Pakistan. In the past decade, my long Foreign Service career was capped by service as U.S. Ambassador to Pakistan (1996–98). That career began the year of my marriage to Peggy Quinn Simons; the marriage and our friendship continue, and for that and all her other munificences my gratitude is almost too deep for words.

Between childhood and career were the university years that were perhaps most critical of all as groundwork for this book. As a Ph.D. candidate in history at Harvard in 1958–60, I read Islamic history in the Classical Age, the first centuries after the Prophet Muhammad, with a great historian, Sir Hamilton A. R. Gibb.

He died in 1971, but his scholarship is still respected and controversial, and his way of approaching the past—straightforward, honest, confident that it makes a difference—remains important for me today. I dedicate this book, as I dedicated the lectures from which it springs, to his memory.

Finally, I would like to thank my editors at Stanford University Press, Amanda Moran, Tim Roberts, and Kate Wahl. Without their professional skill and personal goodwill, the ingredients of what follows, which were there when we met, would have disappeared into thin air.

ISLAM IN A GLOBALIZING WORLD

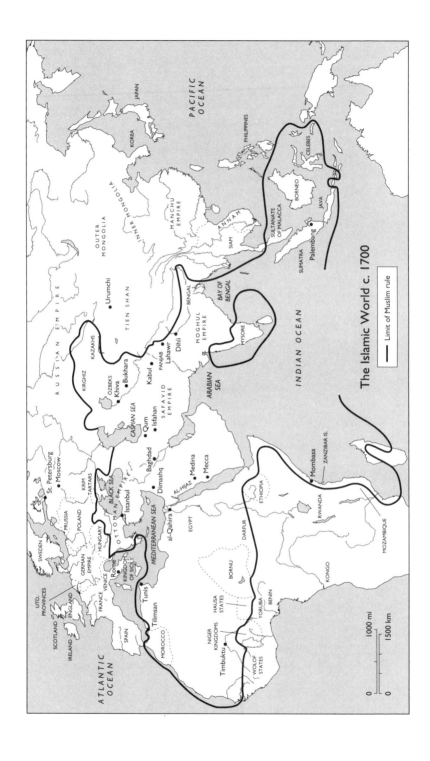

The Islamic World c. 1700

— Limit of Muslim rule

The First Thousand Years: Islam as Globalizer

This small book offers some reflections on the large topic of Islam in a constantly globalizing world, from its beginnings in the seventh century of the Common Era until today. The approach will be historical, based on the assumption that it is not possible to understand today's dilemmas involving Muslims without reference to the millennium and a half of experience from which those dilemmas emerge. But that means selecting, radically simplifying, and taking some risks. Islam is comprehensive in the divine and human questions it asks, almost comprehensive in the range of answers it gives, and forbidding in the length and breadth of human experience it embodies. You can find in it—in its sacred texts and in its experiences—almost anything you want to find in it. So, almost anything you say about Islam will be debatable. Moreover, most statements about Islam have always been highly politicized. That has been true since there was an Islam. It was true in the premodern era, when the statements were usually weapons of religious controversy. It has been true in the modern era, the era of domination and subordination, of Orientalism in the West and of (the more recently baptized) "Occidentalism" in the East.[1] Here it will be assumed that a religion, and hence Islam, "is" what human beings make of it at any given time, as fairly and dispassionately as we can define that shifting target.[2]

This chapter will look briefly at Islam's first millennium. Roughly a thousand years passed between the death of the Prophet Muhammad, in 632 of the Common Era, and (to take convenient turning points) the 1580 truce in the Mediterranean wars between the Vienna-based Habsburgs and the Istanbul-based Ottomans that defined the boundaries, still intact, between Muslim and Christian societies around that sea; or the 1639 treaty of Qasr Shirin, between the Ottomans and the Safavid rulers of Iran, which drew the modern boundary between Iran and Iraq; or the second Ottoman siege of Vienna in 1683, the last high-water mark of Ottoman advance into the center of Europe.

The last date was around the time when, on the shores of Massachusetts Bay, Cotton Mather and Jonathan Edwards were wrestling so strenuously with the omnipotence of God and the sinfulness of man. At the end of Islam's first millennium, religion may have been a defining factor everywhere, but clearly there was a difference in scale between the stakes and resources in play in the Islamic and Transatlantic worlds. At that point, in the sixteenth and seventeenth centuries, Muslims certainly had no reason to feel downhearted about their ability to compete, in either divine or human terms, in "globalization": they were fully competitive.

Since communism fell from power in the late 1980s to

early 1990s, "globalization" has emerged as one common denominator in analyses of world affairs, and it has been given many meanings. Here it is defined as the impulse among humans to reach and go above and beyond the families and kinship groups that historically have provided their first self-definition and best security; to multiply and strengthen their ties via interactions with other human beings; and to argue about why they should or should not do these things. At any given time, globalization has limits set by the state of technology, social organization, and conceptualization, and by the costs it imposes and the resistance it provokes. How far and fast globalization extends, how deeply it penetrates, are functions of the balance between impulse and resistance— but both are always there.

By that definition, during its first millennium Islam was the world's most powerful engine, agent, and vehicle of globalization, and it was also globalization's most sharply contested battleground. That millennium provided Muslims with the golden ages to which they have looked back ever since. It also gave them the strengths and weaknesses they took into the modern world, which was being born as that first millennium ended and which has produced our dilemmas of today.

All the great societies of those thousand years— whether Christian, Hindu, or Chinese—shared certain features with what was becoming the Islamic world. All lived in agricultural economies from which rulers based in cities extracted and spent surpluses in ways that generally had religious sanction. Such rule was usually absolute in theory, but in practice it was limited in range and social impact.

Some features of the Islamic world, however, were unique, not shared with other societies, and of these two stand out. First, every great religious revelation contains something irreducible, which cannot be explained by sociology or development. The Prophet Muhammad's original message that there is but one God was extraordinarily plain, powerful, and rigorous, even compared to Judaism and Christianity, the monotheistic religions it claimed to subsume and supersede. And it was expressed in a specific language, Arabic, a language of exceptional beauty and poetic power.

Second, the geographic area which became the heartland of Islam is also different from others. The central zone over which Islam spread from Arabia, from the Nile to the Oxus in Central Asia, happens to be semi-arid, a region of limited agricultural land separated by large dry areas. Much more than the experience of Christians in forested and rainy Europe, or of Jews in their cities, the Islamic experience therefore has been dominated by the contrast between "the desert and the sown," as the Persian poet Omar Khayyam (1048–ca. 1125 C.E.) put it. Nomadic pastoralists have always been more of a presence in Islam, and more of a problem.[3]

This first millennium was then divided, in terms of Muslim experience, into three main periods.

The first three centuries after the Prophet's death in 632 constitute the Classical Age, the favorite golden age of Muslims. The small Muslim community the Prophet had established in the Arabian merchant cities of Mecca and Medina not only survived the death of its charismatic leader, but immediately embarked on astounding expansion under the so-called four Righteous Caliphs, companions of Muhammad who succeeded him as leaders. They were all from the Meccan clan of the Quraysh. To be sure, the Islamic message was universal, addressed to everyone, but the Islamic *community* was led by men from a specific kinship group. Within a few years they were in charge of Syria, Egypt, much of North Africa, Iraq, and Persia. The Sassanian empire of Persia was destroyed, and the Eastern Roman emperors, the Byzantines, were driven back into Anatolia, the peninsula that is now Turkey.

Unity then broke down in civil wars over the succession to the fourth caliph, Muhammad's cousin and son-in-law 'Ali, who was murdered in 661. It was restored only after a fashion under a dynasty also derived from the Quraysh, the Umayyads, who moved the capital to Damascus in Syria. A dispute over community leadership gradually became the schism dividing the majority Sunnis, followers of Muhammad's sunnah, or path, and the minority Shi'a, partisans of 'Ali. The details of these civil wars have remained extraordinarily vivid in the Islamic imagination: many of today's issues are still debated by Muslims in seventh-century terms.

For the next century the Umayyads consolidated the community and its new empire, using Byzantine and Sassanian models and practices. Islam functioned largely as an Arab-ruled successor state to these great Middle Eastern empires. But this in turn evoked the resentment not just of its new non-Arab subjects, but of the tribal Bedouin Arabs who constituted most of its soldiery. As everywhere in the premodern world, these resentments often took a religious form. So, in 750 C.E., the Umayyads were overthrown and replaced by another dynasty, descended from Muhammad's uncle 'Abbas, which was still Arab and Qurayshi but more broadly based, with its main capital at Baghdad. For the next two centuries these 'Abbasid caliphs presided over the elaboration of a new civilization, in which Hellenistic and Persian traditions were absorbed and also Islamized. It was this period that witnessed the construction of Islam's magnificent spiritual and intellectual architecture. The text of the divine message Muhammad had received, the Qur'an, was more or less fixed in its current form within two decades of his death. The compilation and authentication of the vast body of his sayings—the *hadith*, or traditions—was substantially complete within two centuries. And by then the elaboration from both these sources of the divine law of the community, the *shari'a*, was also well underway. Great systems of jurisprudence, or *fiqh*, arose: most Sunnis followed four of these; Shi'a had *fiqh* systems of their own. These achievements provided the soul and much of the structure for an empire that was glorious for its power, culture, and wealth; it was the fabulous civilization we associate with the *Arabian Nights*.

Yet this was also the civilization of a dominant but vulnerable minority. It was ruled by Arab Muslim dynasties, but throughout these three centuries most of the *people* in this Muslim empire remained Christian, Jewish, or Zoroastrian. So the integration of Hellenistic, Persian, and Arab traditions and their Islamization remained very much an elite phenomenon. And that fact, in turn, helps explain the enormous stress in Islam on the unity of the community of Muslims, the *umma*.

The high value attached to Muslim unity was as old as the *umma* itself, since it began as an embattled small group around the Prophet in Mecca and Medina. But now that Muslims constituted a minority ruling a large empire, the unity of their *umma* took on a religious value only scarcely less urgent than the unity of God.

Moreover, the course of events also lent the riveting power of the ideal not just to the unity of the community, but also to the indivisibility of religion and politics in Islam. For the Prophet and his immediate successors, and the Muslims gathered around them, there was no distinction to be made between spiritual and secular authority. But now the civil wars of the fourth decade forced a separation in practice of the religious and political powers. Political authority in the Islamic lands was never again to be uncontested on religious grounds. But the shock of the separation was great, and once again the ideal was called upon to fill the chasm that had opened up in reality. The horror at disunity which the civil wars had provoked forever soldered religion and politics together in Islamic theory and belief.

Finally, tribal pastoralists were a problem from the beginning. Muhammad and the first caliphs were city people, but their conquering armies were drawn from the Bedouins around them. Newly converted, these Bedouins were unruly and prone to discontent, and that discontent most often took religious form. It was among them, and from the beginning, that the call for a radical return to the purity of the original Islamic message and the first community resonated most strongly.

At the height of 'Abbasid power, in the mid-ninth century, the caliph al-Ma'mun sought to arrogate to himself the authority to make religious decisions. The attempt was squelched by the scholars and their supporters in the city crowds, and basically it was never seriously repeated. So, after all, the religious and political authorities were shown to be separate. But this also meant that the scholars henceforth defined a ruler's Islamic legitimacy purely in terms of his personal and Islamic virtues. Concept and law alike stressed relations among individuals rather than among or between groups. So long as 'Abbasid rule was strong, it was easy to assume that the private and public obligations of Muslims coincided. But the assumption was vulnerable to power shifts: without centralized monarchy aspiring to universality, it was hard to legitimate political power in Islamic terms. No wonder developing Islamic discourse was sophisticated, nervous, and lively in these centuries: it was dancing on the lips of volcanoes. Looking back, however, it is also true that the integrated, comprehensive Islam that Islamic discourse fashioned in these years was a triumph of the human spirit, and that is what it remains today.

Over time 'Abbasid rule ceased to be strong. Beginning in the ninth century, and increasingly thereafter, it came under pressure from pastoralists inside and outside the empire. Bedouins emerged once more from the Arabian Peninsula, and Turks came in from Central Asia. Like the Romans with the Germans, the 'Abbasids first tried to coopt these warrior nomads by hiring them as mercenaries, and then found themselves taken over by them. In the mid-tenth century, after two centuries of 'Abbasid rule, the 'Abbasid caliph in Baghdad was reduced to a figurehead by the Persian warrior dynasty of the Buyids, with its mountaineer and Turkish troops; and Turks kept coming. The destruction of Baghdad by the even fiercer Mongols in 1258 should have been the culmination, but it was not: the migrations really culminated only with Timur, our Tamerlane, with his Central Asian empire and his mountains of skulls, around 1400.

Agriculture and the cities that depended on it deteriorated. Religious orthodoxy was threatened too. The religious radicalism that came naturally to predatory nomadic warriors could be Shi'a, and by the tenth and eleventh centuries most rulers in the old central zone were Shi'a. Beginning in the eleventh century, this incipient Shi'i ascendancy was aborted by an intricately interwoven combination of Sunni revival and an upsurge of the newer mysticism of the Sufis, the search for personal union with God that took the believer away from worldly complexity and pain. Sufis now organized themselves in orders with distinct practices and leadership lineages of holy *pir*s and sheikhs. And while Sufism appealed to almost everyone, these orders appealed especially to Turks. Sufism tended easily toward pantheism, the belief that God is everywhere at once and nowhere in particular. While it was associated with the Sunni revival, Sufism was a mixed blessing for Sunni orthodoxy: it allowed the structure built around the *shari'a* to stand intact, but seemed always on the verge of hollowing it out from within until it collapsed.

Yet the religious "institution" survived where centralized political authority did not. These were also the centuries when the masses were converted to Islam for the first time, when the Islamic world became *Muslim* for the first time, and when Islam expanded to the ends of the known earth: to India, from there to Southeast Asia and the Indies, and, on the other side, to Africa. Much missionary work was done by Sufis, holy men clearing land in the jungles and converting the pagans and animists into new Muslim communities. In Eastern India and the African interior, Islam was in fact associated with the transition from hunting and gathering to settled agriculture—or, in other words, with an earlier stage of globalization.[4] But the *religious* result was an extraordinary latitudinarianism, huge laxity when it came to actual beliefs. To expand, Islam swallowed pre-Islamic beliefs and practices in order to transform them. And like political disunity, this "broadness" threatened to dissolve Islam as an integrated religion, faithful to the original message God had conveyed through the Prophet.

Yet it did survive, and there are two main reasons why.

The first was the extraordinary Sunni revival of the tenth and eleventh centuries. The Shi'i rulers and the Sufi allies were threats to Sunni orthodoxy, but they also stimulated Sunni energy and renewal. In just a few generations of splendid devotional and intellectual effort, scholars built a superb new synthesis of *shari'a* and Sufism, law and mysticism, which permitted the *'ulama*, the religious scholars, to live and work together for the faith with the sheikhs and *pir*s of Sufism.

Second, this new synthesis was then extended to the political sphere by the Turkic dynasty of the Seljuqs, which dominated the central lands of Islam in the century and a half around 1100. It combined military dynasties, Sunni *'ulama*, and the Sufi orders, a combination that remained characteristic of the Islamic world for the next four centuries. To rise above the original tribal basis of most of these dynasties, there arose the practice of recruiting boys from among non-Islamic peoples, converting them to Islam, making them the ruler's personal slaves, and then staffing his military and administrative elites with them, since they were beholden to no one else. It was also in this period that governments established the practice of endowing and supporting religious colleges, the *madrasseh*, that gave structure and continuity to the religious institution.

So an alliance of orthodoxy and some political authority survived. But as in all human affairs, these achievements came at a price. In fact, there were several prices. First, under the new synthesis it proved impossible to restore that coincidence of private and public obligations which 'Abbasid power had allowed Muslims to assume but which 'Abbasid decline had split asunder. In recent years the question of "institutions," and in particular the relationship of Islam and the state, classical, medieval, and modern, has become one of the most vexed and controversial in Islamic studies. Certainly Muslims of every period, including this middle period, had arrangements, habits, and loyalties which protected and defended them and their interests in a hard world, in the same way as Western "institutions" and "basic units of society" worked for Europeans. Of course, groups with rules and structure existed: mosques and schools, guilds, the Sufi orders, the schools of law. They were endowed and managed in accordance with charters, they were supervised by boards. They had "personalities." Muslims identified themselves in varying degrees with "groups," including, but also extending beyond, family and clan. But what Muslims did not have were clear, settled, and durable understandings of how being Muslim or identifying with a group was related to political power.

Hence, beyond the local level, religious legitimation for the ruler became even weaker and more problematic than it had been under the 'Abbasids. Earlier jurists had expatiated upon the Islamic virtues that a just ruler should have. Now, dealing with barely converted warrior chiefs from Turkic clans, scholars took to preaching the religious duty of obedience even to *unjust* rulers, on the ground that disorder was so dangerous to the *umma*, and thus to God's message in the world, that *any* order was preferable: "necessity makes legal what would otherwise not be legal," as the great al-Ghazali put it.[5] Rulers were necessary because without them there could be no justice; but as a rationale for legitimacy this explanation was lame.

And it is also true that over these hard centuries the religious "institution" became extraordinarily conservative. Once again, the question of *how* conservative is highly controversial in modern Islamic scholarship. Certainly, in practice even more than in doctrine, though certainly in doctrine, there always remained a place in Sunni orthodoxy for interpretation and judgment, even for what we (not they) would call innovation. Contrary to a view widespread even among Muslims, the gate of *ijtihad*, of rightful effort to apply law and doctrine to new situations, never swung completely closed; for Shi'a, as an embattled minority, it remained a necessity. *Ijma'*, the consensus of the doctors, was never comprehensive nor wholly enforceable.

In these centuries, nevertheless, order was continually

threatened by religious radicalism, mysticism, and the tribalist nomads to whom they most appealed. Moreover, as the years passed, more and more questions were addressed, discussed, and resolved to the satisfaction of most. For both reasons, religious scholars in their urban citadels were increasingly tempted to hunker down on what had already been achieved. Once the great new Sunni synthesis was in place and Sunnis had become the Islamic majority again, for them the scope for *ijtihad* narrowed significantly. *Ijma'* became weightier; *bida*, innovation, more repugnant. What diversity already existed was accepted as the price of *umma* unity, but at *another* price: rather than ortho*doxy*, conformity in doctrine, mainstream Islam stressed ortho*praxy*, conformity in behavior, and justified it in religious terms. Just as there was still *ijtihad*, there was still diversity in practices, and the more the merrier on the expanding frontiers of the Islamic world; but *ijtihad* and heteropraxy were more and more thrust to the margins of the Islamic ideal.[6]

Then, with another huge turn of history's wheel, came two centuries in which Muslims proved once again that they could go beyond conservatism, that they could rise above the just-emerging conservative consensus in politics and religion. In the years around 1500 the Islamic world witnessed the almost simultaneous rise of three great empires: the Ottomans in Anatolia, southeastern Europe, Egypt, Syria, and then Iraq; the Safavids in Persia; and the Timurids, the dynasty we call the Moghuls, in North India and Afghanistan. As usual with globalization, technological change had something to do with it. In this case it was the widespread use of gunpowder weapons in warfare, weapons that also helped create the

Portuguese and Spanish empires with which they competed: thus they are called the "gunpowder empires." All three dynasties had been around for some time; the Ottomans, for instance, had ruled the Balkans and most of Anatolia since the fourteenth century. All had Turkic origins, and all ruled basically by right of conquest, however much they legitimated their dominion as the keepers of God's law.

There were, of course, differences between these dynasties. The Ottomans and Timurids were Sunni; the Safavids made Iran the Shi'i state and civilization it has remained ever since. But they all developed legitimacies which took them beyond the military patronage states and the simple legitimation from necessity that had marked the previous era. They drew on three different traditions: the Timurids on Mongol prestige and universalism dating back to Genghis Khan; the Safavids on the reforming zeal of Shi'ism in the old Islamic heartland; the Ottomans on the holy warrior sense of community mission on the "bloody borders" of Islam and Christendom.[7] But as time went on each added an Islamic communalist cast that was new, and each managed some integration of the religious establishment into the state power structure. Return to the purity and unity of the original message and the original community always beckoned as an ideal. But these three regimes based themselves on something broader, certainly Islamic but also more than that. In reality, they discovered partial solutions to Islam's classic difficulty of finding religious legitimation for political power.[8]

These Islamic gunpowder empires were polities intermediate between the universal Muslim *umma* of the

Islamic ideal and the military patronage states they had superseded. But like their equally absolutist European contemporaries—the Spain of the Catholic Kings, for instance, or the France of the Most Christian Kings— they demonstrated that a pure form is not required to achieve extraordinary wealth, sophistication, and power. When the Ottomans besieged Vienna in 1683, it was the second time they had done it; they had been there in 1529. They never took it, of course; but the point is that it was they who were besieging Vienna, and not the Habsburgs under the walls of Istanbul.

During its first millennium, then, Islam was at the forefront of whatever globalization mankind could muster in that age, and at the end of that millennium, around 1700, Islam was fully competitive according to the standards of globalization then in force. In other words, in terms of globalization, differences between Islam and other major civilizations made no difference; they did not yet matter in power terms. It was only in the new era then beginning that they came to matter very greatly indeed.

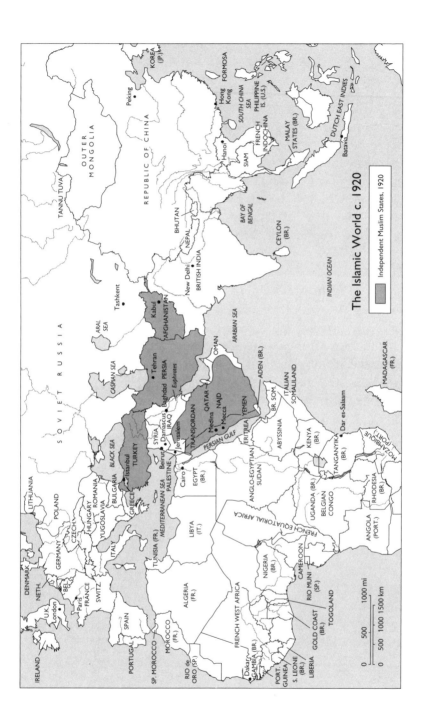

The Islamic World c. 1920

☐ Independent Muslim States, 1920

2

Islam and Globalization by Blood and Iron

The seventeenth century of the Common Era saw the awakening of a world in which much of mankind's impulse toward globalization took on new forms and adopted new means—a process at which non-Muslims eventually proved more adept than Muslims. "Blood and iron" is a nineteenth-century coinage referring to the German empire founded in 1871. But the same phrase could characterize all industrial and military power based on coal and iron, then steel, and then petroleum, the motors for globalization over the next three centuries, and for the territorial nation-state, which was its main vehicle, and for the racism which was often its fuel. "Blood and iron" were central to the type of globalization Muslims grappled with for three centuries, up to our own day, in about 1970, when the globalizing impulse began to take on the newer shapes and contents that we are still trying to understand and control.

Globalization by blood and iron was born at the western end of the small European peninsula. It was commercial before it became industrial. Its impulse was strongest on Europe's Atlantic seaboard, among the English, the Dutch, and the French, whose economies were going beyond the agricultural bases that had underpinned every previous civilization. New ways of thinking were emerging, new ways of setting and pursuing goals and power, and new groups interested in accumulating and maintaining that power. After more than a century of bloody wars fought in the name of religion, there was less and less resorting to religious rationales, to collective definitions of value—although sometimes old ones were replaced by new ones. Increasingly, the concepts of reason and the individual framed thought and action. In politics, there was less reference to Christendom and more to the nation, less to dynasty and more to the state.

What is striking for the next century and a half, however, is not how much these developments mattered to Muslims, but how little. As they had when the Grand Vizier Kara Mustapha pitched his tent before Vienna, most Muslims continued to live in the three gunpowder empires; their dynasties ruled agricultural societies absolutely with some religious legitimation; and each benefited from the magnificent intellectual and institutional edifice built up in Islam over the previous millennium.

There were permanent regressive and revivalist streaks within the edifice. The century of origins, our seventh century, remained a strong point of reference; there was always a nostalgia for the mythologized unity and purity of the early community. The edifice also had great inertial weight, a strong religious conservatism born of earlier turmoil and vulnerability. But it was also true that radical return to a mythical age of origins appealed

mainly to the more marginal elements in Islamic societies: to Bedouins and other tribals, to vulnerable small
people in the cities, if they could not find spiritual
homes in the Sufi orders. Mainstream Islam, most of the
real *umma*, the actual community of believers, had gone
and for the most part remained far beyond them. All
three of the main empires had achieved a partial integration of religious and political institutions, and had bases
of legitimacy that included Islam but went beyond it.

Into the early years of the nineteenth century, then,
most Muslims continued to march very much to their
own drummers. Of course there was contact and inter-
action; of course the emergence of the modern in its
West European forms mattered to Muslims in some
ways. The empires they lived in were in trouble, and
European pressure increased their troubles. Efforts to
reequip and strengthen the Ottoman state for stouter
resistance began early in the eighteenth century. But
now Habsburg armies moved south through the Balkans, the Russians toward the Black Sea, the British
across the Ganges Plain and then through the Deccan
Peninsula in India. In 1798 the French under Napoleon
took Egypt, until the British and the Ottomans drove
them out and installed the reformist governor Muhammad (Mehmet) 'Ali. The military momentum was shifting toward the West. It was not the only factor. There
was always trade, and producing for Europe could bring
social change and tension that had political consequences: some of Muhammad 'Ali's support came from
"new men" in Egyptian society.[1]

Yet very little changed in the Islamic world as a result,
and a good deal changed without any reference at all to

the modern world taking shape in Europe. The eighteenth century in the Islamic world was in fact a kind of silver age, a century of important developments in many regions, from Morocco to the Indies. And these developments were rooted in indigenous impulses, including Islamic impulses.

To be sure, political power dispersed, out from the old centers to provincial governors and local notables who turned their delegated authorities into new sovereignties. But the lands they ruled were not necessarily less secure, nor were the economies less productive than before. And in intellectual and religious life the movement was in the other direction: toward renewal. The impulse to renewal and reform appeared almost simultaneously in a number of disparate places in the Islamic world. There has been lively scholarly discussion about the degree of linkage among these new developments. For some, the impulse centered on the Holy Cities Mecca and Medina, in Arabia, and the localities where scholars traveling to and from them met, Egypt and south Arabia.[2] Other scholars argue that diverse local roots and causes were more critical, that "network" is basically a misnomer. In India, where Muslims were a minority among Hindus and where the Moghul central power that had protected and promoted them decayed with great speed, new purity and integrity seemed needed more than elsewhere; so Indian scholars like Shah Wali Ullah of Delhi were in the forefront of change.[3] But it is also true that scholars from all over the Islamic world contributed to a new stress on asceticism and piety; a new focus on God's transcendence; and new bases for religious authority, with *ijtihad* now defined as an obligation for every believer rather than the preserve of the schools.[4] And Sufism moved in the same directions; a revived and reinvigorated Naqshbandiyya order of Sufis had a special role to play.[5] The stress on God's transcendence not only served to insulate Islam from other religions, it brought Muslims together by lifting Sufism's mystical impulse up from the mire of pantheism. In Egypt, a deepening of Sufi piety and a revival of logical reasoning in theology went hand in hand, a kind of miniature eighteenth-century version of the great Sunni revival six centuries before.[6] The effect was to create new coalitions of *'ulama* and the masses.

These developments represented globalization of a kind: they could probably not have taken place without improved means of communication, and the new coalitions within society diluted Islam's elitism. Just how broad and healthy eighteenth-century change was is shown by its extreme: the Wahhabi movement, named after the scholar Muhammad ibn 'Abd al-Wahhab, which arose in the Arabian desert late in the century and forged an alliance with the tribal leadership of the House of Sa'ud. Together they managed to overrun the Holy Cities before being expelled by the Egyptians back to their desert fastnesses. Wahhabism turned the century's ascetic and purifying impulse into a call for radical and exclusivist return to the simplicity and unity of the seventh century. This had some plausibility in the center of Arabia, but little if any in places like India, where Muslims lived as a minority and had to compromise and "reason together" if they were to survive as Muslims. The Wahhabi movement, in other words, remained what such movements had always been in Islam: good enough for Bedouins and very few others.[7]

By the early nineteenth century, nevertheless, it finally

came about that the pressure from a transformed and hugely strengthened Europe loomed as an increasingly important fact of life for the old centers of the Islamic world and their leaderships. The impact was not uniform or comprehensive. Most Muslims lived as they had; most changes were still self-generated. But by 1820 to 1840, for more and more Muslims, Western pressure, encroachment, and penetration had become the central fact of public life. Simplifying as we must, we can say Muslims responded in three main ways.

The first was top-down modernization by the elites. They adopted, introduced, imposed Western techniques, methods, and concepts in order to improve their capacity to compete with the West without sacrificing what was most precious and essential of their own. In the Ottoman lands, in Egypt, the program included recentralization of political authority: the dispersion of power of the eighteenth century, in other words, was reversed. It included land reform, legal reform to provide for state law and the equality of all citizens before it, and the centralization of fiscal and budget authorities. In colonial areas, these reforms were often imposed directly by the Western colonial authorities, as in British India, or in Algeria under France after 1830. The reforms created in Islamic societies the modern concepts of the "citizen" and of the "economy" separate from the state. But the reformers in fact were fixated on the state. Often the language of reform and innovation was Islamic. But with so many measures being taken off the shelf from European experience, it was still hard to escape the charge that top-down reform was imported and *un*-Islamic.

Precisely to avoid being tarred with a Western or infi-

del brush, an allied set of reformers tried to adapt Islam
to the Western values they were espousing. These adaptationists were often people created by reform, for whom
there was no going back. They were the new professionals, whose Western education equipped them to staff the
new armies and bureaucracies, the new owners of large,
and now often private, agricultural holdings. Previously
most land had been held from the state, so that new
large private property was actually a novelty, an innovation. In Egypt, within half a century after the introduction of long-staple cotton in 1821, much of the Nile delta
had turned into one large plantation producing for the
world market. And these landowners wanted their children to have Western education—and the job opportunities it created. These new men and their families were
usually pious Muslims, but they also lived by and
accepted Western norms and values. At bottom, their
vision for Islamic societies projected Western trajectories
to Western outcomes, and especially the modern, powerful nation-state. But they wished to justify their adap-
tations in Islamic terms.[8]

Third, there were the resisters, who very often also
justified their resistance in terms of Islam. As new kinds
of modernizing change penetrated and spread, more and
more Muslims sought some combination of continuity
and adaptation. Not all resistance took Messianic or
apocalyptic forms, but some did. Some (among the
Shi'a) were tempted by archaic hopes of the return of
the Imam, who had been hidden or occluded since the
ninth century. Others yearned for the coming of the
Mahdi, the Rightly Guided One who would impose
righteousness just before the Last Judgment.[9] Or the

longed-for event could be the end of the world itself, the Judgment Day that had been so important to the Prophet. These utopias had been around almost from the beginning. Now, some resisters constructed new versions of the old dream of return to the purity of the original *umma*. For example, once the Ottoman Caliphate was abolished in the 1920s by the Turkish state, the dream of reestablishing it also became a kind of utopia, as it is to this day.[10] But now these utopias appealed not just to Bedouins or peasants, but also to the city mob, to the growing groups of city artisans and small traders for whom Western economic forms threatened social degradation.

So long as modernity in its European form had the wind in its sails, resistance appeared futile even when it was heroic, commanded by God. And as long as European domination seemed solid, top-down modernization and nationalism—joining the West in order to compete with it—were simply more plausible than resistance. In fact, they achieved a good deal of modernization, but that achievement has been labeled a "simulacrum of modernity"; what was put in place, it is argued, was false, or sham, or too partial to be the real thing.[11] And it is true that in practical terms, on the face of things, modernity of this kind affected only some parts of the Islamic world, only some Muslims, and only to some degree. In particular, it began as an elite phenomenon and trickled down only imperfectly. So calling it a simulacrum of modernity has some plausibility.

However, it can be argued just as strongly that all *three* responses—including Islamicized resistance—were in fact modern.[12] Compared to what had gone before, all three responses in fact partook of modernity, were framed in essentially modern terms, and implied essentially modern categories of thought and action. In terms of understanding the experience of Muslims, the effect is to reverse the argument: rather than a simulacrum of modernity, what the Islamic world got instead was a simulacrum of *unmodernity*. In other words it became modern but could not admit it: to themselves, many Muslims have tried to pass—against the evidence—as still premodern.

Modernity certainly had a growing economic base. The key areas of the Islamic world were increasingly geared to a world economic system dominated by the West; the West's economic cycles became the Islamic world's cycles. It was true that they often had effects on Islamic societies different from the effects elsewhere. In particular, the changes they inflicted there did not produce durable mass social and political movements as they had in Europe. Repression, the hugeness of peasantries and the smallness of cities, elite fears of popular savagery, the enormous inertial strength of "society" and the orthopraxy underpinning it: all help explain why. Joel Beinin recounts that during the Arab Revolt in Palestine in the 1930s, insurrectionary peasants took some small towns for a while and immediately imposed the long dress on women and the peasant cap on men in place of the fez.[13] But if the mix of causes was local, the result was everywhere the same: the new movements that emerged to support modernization were rather small and mainly elite phenomena.

In their limited ambits, nevertheless, the three responses to Western pressure basically replicated the political categories of modernizing Europe in Islamic terms. Beyond simple traditionalists, Europe had its liberals, its nationalists, and its social revolutionaries. So too with the Islamic world: in addition to traditionalists, it had its top-down modernizers, equivalent to European liberals; its adaptationist landowners and professionals, equivalent to European nationalists; and its religious radicals, equivalent to European social revolutionaries.[14] Even more significantly, just as in Europe, all these Muslims took the nation-state as their point of reference, positive or negative. Traditionalist radicals might wish to use the state to hasten the Last Judgment or recreate the original *umma*; more modernist radicals might wish to imbue the state with Islam and use it to enforce the *shari'a*. But like the Europeans, none had a real frame of reference other than the nation-state.[15] As with their European contemporaries, therefore, transcendence drained slowly out of their lives and societies, and was replaced by the will to power. And that was modern too.[16]

Yet because of Western domination, the growing modernism of Islamic societies could not be recognized and be called what it was. Because of Western domination, everything or almost everything had to be described in Islamic terms. Western pressure forced everything into Islamic language. Moreover, Islamicizing everything was also part of Westernization itself. For the great body of Western scholarship, knowledge, and propaganda about the Islamic world *also* insisted that what distinguished these societies from the West—for good or ill—was, precisely, Islam: an Islam rooted in the seventh century and mired in the fourteenth, an Islam that made no distinction between religion and politics, an Islam incompatible with modernization.

And the inability of Muslims to call their modernity by its name bore a high cost. For it brought with it a progressive simplification and brutalization of the Islamic discourse. As Western domination spread and deepened in the late nineteenth century, its engine was superior military power, overt or in the background. But it was justified in terms of culture, religion, and race; and it was accompanied by a coarsening of European discourse, an increasing rawness and nastiness in intellectual and political life. In Europe and the United States this was the era of social Darwinism and the new mass parties and new imperialist mass publics. And as it modernized in its turn, the Islamic world to the south and east of Europe produced its *own* version of that same coarsening.

The Islamic public was limited, to be sure. Until the 1960s the great majority of Muslims remained peasants; Muslim cities were islands in peasant seas. Muslim intellectuals were even more isolated than intellectuals in the West. Men like Jamal ad-Din al-Afghani, Muhammad 'Abduh, or Rashid Rida lived embattled lives, intellectually and morally. As they struggled, they too were tempted to leave behind the refinement and the sophistication of eighteenth-century Islam in favor of slogans, semi-ideologies, and formulas.[17] As a result, all these impulses were basically modern, but the liberals had bad consciences, the nationalists were crippled by Western domination and *obbligato* Islamic language, and the social revolutionaries had no real basis for action in society. The effect on radicals was particularly crippling, for their seventh-century language and ideals omitted the real object of their struggle: the state, which alone could provide Muslims with a modicum of emancipation and then with a modicum of justice.

World War I was a turning point for Muslims, even if it seemed at the time to consolidate Western domination. The main Western forces at work in the Islamic world were British and French, and Britain and France were among the victors. But they were wounded and depleted even in victory. Their dominion now seemed less inevitable; emancipation became conceivable; and with it came the hope that Muslims could go beyond the truncations and prevarications that came with their subordination.

For the time being it was not to be. In the central, mainly Arab lands, the Ottoman collapse left the British and French in charge, in collaboration with nationalist landowners and army officers. Only in Turkey, with its peasant-farmer majority and a population that, in the wake of Ottoman defeat, associated religion with national treachery, was it possible to establish a nation-state that was not dependent on Western patronage. Even under strong modernizers, Iran and Afghanistan could take only half steps in the same direction. The Western shadow was heavy everywhere else, and deepened as Western industry began the switch from coal to oil and new oil reserves were discovered in the Middle East. For modernizing Muslim elites, the lesson of the interwar years was that their only real option was simply to expel the foreigners and take over the colonial state.

By the interwar period, it is true, development was producing a drift of people from the country to the city which created mixed populations torn from their country roots but not yet comfortable with modernity. They were even producing their own voices: Hasan al-Banna, founder of the Muslim Brotherhood in Egypt in 1928, born a peasant; Sayyid Qutb, who carried on after Hasan was assassinated in 1949, already born in the city. Both rejected the nation-state on principle. But like their fellow Islamist radical in India, Maulana Abu-l-'Ala Maududi, they mainly wanted to take over the state for Islam. The radical revivalism that had always been associated with Bedouins was now moving into the cities, and was beginning to find a modern idiom and timbre.[18]

For the time being, such voices remained marginal. World War II was another, still more violent caesura, for this time France was actually defeated (for a while), and Britain, while victorious again, was exhausted. The two decades after the war's end saw astonishingly swift formal decolonization, first in Asia, then in the Middle East, last of all in Africa. Islamic societies were also swept up in this great movement. The postwar years brought a cascade of liberation between Syria and Lebanon in 1944 and Algeria in 1962. Yet liberation did not take place under radical or revivalist auspices. In most Muslim countries the process was dominated by coalitions of Westernized intellectuals and army officers drawn from the countryside. And the dominant ideology of this decolonization movement was republican nationalism with an Islamic admixture.[19]

This religiously tinged nationalism among Muslims was all the more riveting because it was the mirror image and antidote to the State of Israel, which also combined religion and nationality. Israel's anchorage in the heart of the Islamic world from 1948 onward was a continual challenge and reminder to Muslims that formal emancipation had not brought freedom from subordination. But had Israel not been a sworn enemy, their republican nationalism might have found a twin in the Labor Zionism that presided over the birth of the new state.

Most of the Islamic public was affected by some form of this republican nationalism. In the Arab world the form was the "Arab socialism" associated with Egyptian leader Gamal 'Abd al-Nasser. This was a package of state-led national development, composed of import-substitution industrialization, land reform, and modern education and social welfare. With land reform, Nasser (and later Muhammad Reza Shah of Iran) succeeded in destroying the landowners as contestants for political primacy in the nationalist camp.[20] But since neither ruler was willing to empower the peasant majorities, the result for each was a bloated bureaucratic state within a political framework dominated by single parties and policemen.

Moreover, most countries with Muslim majorities had few significant natural resources for competition in the burgeoning postwar world economy, except for oil and gas. As Professor Terry Karl has argued, oil and gas are special as commodities, different from iron and steel, because exploiting them does not necessarily force broad changes in society and politics. Making oil the engine of growth does not necessarily create new working classes and new middle classes, and its profits can easily be captured by the elites already in place.[21] As it happened, the postwar oil bonanza in the Muslim world occurred mainly in conservative monarchies: the Gulf emirates, Iran, and especially Saudi Arabia. Oil also increasingly drove economic growth for the Western side of the Cold

War led by the United States. So for all the tension between them over Israel, the monarchies and the West were soldered together, so to speak, by oil.

As it also happened, the countries that did not have oil were those where republican nationalism was strongest: Egypt, Syria, and South Yemen. Iraq was something of an anomaly, for it had oil but after 1958 was a republic; so was Algeria, when it gained access to its burgeoning production after independence. But for Egypt, Syria, and Yemen, the only alternative to the oil they did not have was "Arab socialist" development supported by Cold War alliances with the Second World, the Soviet Union and its allies. After the Suez crisis of 1956, history indeed appeared to be on Arab socialism's side under Nasser. But as oil revenues began to spiral, the Saudis started to create an alternative camp within the Islamic world. By the mid-1960s they were legitimating their side of the struggle more and more with Islamic revivalism, updated from the Wahhabism that had accompanied them since the eighteenth century.

This in turn forced Nasser to fight his patch more and more in Islamic terms. As a result, the false consciousness that European domination stamped onto Islamic discourse persisted into the postcolonial Islamic world. The *issues* of engagement were increasingly economic and political, but the *terms* of engagement were increasingly Islamic. It was, after all, a struggle between those Muslims who had and those who did not have oil to support growth and validate their rule; but it was described as a contest between republican nationalism and revivalism under monarchical auspices. And that in turn locked the Islamic world into continued bad faith.

Colonialism was now past, but because the Islamic archaism which colonialism had fostered was fastened onto Islamic societies like a succubus, it was still too soon for the modern nation-state.

The Egyptian-Saudi competition that began in the 1960s heated up against the backdrop of two momentous historical shifts that were getting underway simultaneously. First, the costs of state-led development in capital-short economies were beginning to rise dramatically. Two in particular were linked: state-led industrialization shortchanged and ran down agriculture, and this produced waves of new rural out-migration to the cities. Second, growth and power in the international system were coming to depend less on commodities, whether coal, steel, or oil, and more on information technology and knowledge. For Muslims, that new stage would bring great new dangers and great new opportunities.

3

Comparative Radicalisms, 1870–1970

> Mon crime est atroce, et il fut *prémédité*. J'ai donc mérité la mort, Messieurs les jurés. Mais quand je serais moins coupable, je vois des hommes qui, sans s'arrêter à ce que ma jeunesse peut mériter de pitié, voudront punir en moi et décourager à jamais cette classe de jeunes gens qui, nés dans une classe inférieure et en quelque sorte opprimés par la pauvreté, ont le bonheur de se procurer une bonne éducation, et l'audace de se mêler à ce que l'orgueil des gens riches appelle la société.*
>
> Julien Sorel to his jury, Stendhal,
> *Le Rouge et le noir* (1830)

The years around 1970 were the real starting point for the intricate, winding paths that led some thirty years later to the stupefying attacks on the World Trade Towers and the Pentagon on September 11, 2001. As the foregoing has suggested, in some ways one can also legitimately start with the seventh century or the seventeenth. But the true point of origin is in our own time. These origins are quite specific: they involve particular choices made by men and women in particular circumstances. And yet they also recall choices and developments in Russia and Eastern Europe a century earlier. Comparing the two times is not to argue that they are the same; it is to help us understand our own. And most especially, it may help us understand the young men who burst forth from the shadows so unexpectedly and so devastatingly just after the start of the new millennium.

The young of both times and places—the Russian world after 1870 and the Arab world around 1970—were seared by the frustration of always living second-rate lives in relation to those at the cutting edge of globalization. There are tremendous penalties for latecomers to the modernization sweepstakes. If sustained development doubles income in twenty years, then starting twenty years late means that, although your economy's income has doubled in two decades, the front-runner's has already quadrupled. As it happened, countries like Romania or Bulgaria actually fell *further* behind Western Europe in the nineteenth century.[1] But whether a late-starting country is advancing or slipping back in relative economic terms, it is *always* behind; and this reality is always painful, and the pain often is felt most keenly not by the poorest, but by those who have progressed a little and are frustrated in their aspirations to go further. Some want to catch up entirely: Nikita Khrushchev provided a late example for his region when he announced in 1961 that the Soviet Union would overtake the United States economically by 1980. Others, like some of the Islamists of our times, despair at *ever* catching up in Western terms, and try to shift the terms of the competition.

This chapter will focus on exactly who those people were in the Islamic world around 1970, and will compare them to similar people in the European East starting around 1870. For Europe the focus will be on Russia, for the Islamic world on its Arab regions. This is partly because the data are better for these (our situation is reminiscent of the man who had lost a quarter and looked under a streetlamp a block away because there was more light). Mainly, however, this will be our strategy because, to paraphrase scripture, trouble must needs come, but woe unto him by whom the trouble cometh. While radical socialism was endemic to the whole European East a century or so ago, it came to power in Russia; and while the radicalism we have come to call Political Islam has taken hold in a number of places, it has been very much a product of the Arab world.[2]

THE ISLAMIC HEARTLANDS AROUND 1970

In the Arab regions, the years around 1970 rang the death knell on the high hopes that had accompanied the decolonization process. From the 1940s into the 1960s many Arabs had felt they were on the threshold of freedom, prosperity, and dignity. Republican nationalism, even when it went under the name of the Arab socialism associated with Egyptian leader Gamal 'Abd al-Nasser, had given the best ideological shape to these hopes. It basically accepted the territorial state established by and inherited from the colonizers, but sought to give it a broader and especially nonmonarchical content. Surviving the 1956 Suez invasion against Britain, France, and Israel had made Nasser by far the most commanding political leader in the area. Like all others he gave his ideology an Islamic tinge and language, but "Arab socialism" in practice supported a program of extending state control over society by state-led development with three main components: industrialization focused on substituting for imported manufactures, land reform taking land from landowners and giving it to peasants, and expanded education and social welfare.[3]

From its foundation in 1948, Israel had been a constant reminder that the end of colonialism need not mean the end of subordination, and the oil boom and the Cold War together had clouded prospects still further. But in the competition for allies and influence between republican Egypt and monarchical Saudi Arabia, a competition that gathered steam in the 1960s, there was no preordained victor or political result. There was nothing inevitable about the Islamist tide that rose around 1970 to threaten both: it resulted from specific socioeconomic and political developments during these years.

There were real accomplishments in industrialization. Outside oil and gas, development focused on consumer goods: food products, building materials, and textiles. Between 1960 and 1980 the percentage of the labor force employed in industry and manufacturing increased in Egypt from 12 percent to 30 percent, from 19 to 31 percent in Syria, from 23 to 34 percent in Iran, and from 10 to 14 percent even in Saudi Arabia.[4] To have a third of the labor force in industry is really to have modernized.

But it is also true that this industrialization was heavily based on oil. If the contribution of oil and gas is subtracted from total industrial production, industry's contribution to Gross Domestic Product (GDP) fell from 44 percent to 4.2 percent in Algeria and from 74 percent to 1.5 percent in Saudi Arabia.[5] Compared to coal and steel, as mentioned in the last chapter, oil and gas are special commodities, in the sense that exploiting them does not force the creation of large labor forces or large middle classes, and the profits from oil and gas are easily captured by the elites already in place.[6] So it was in the Islamic heartlands.

Moreover, to achieve even this degree of industrialization the agricultural sector was substantially sacrificed. Never extremely prosperous in this semi-arid zone, agriculture was tapped by governments for the resources needed to industrialize, either through direct taxation or through overvalued currencies that made traditional agricultural exports more expensive and imports less so. To take a few examples from this period, between 1960 and 1981 agricultural output as a percentage of GDP dropped almost everywhere: from 30 percent to 21 percent in Egypt, from 24 to 16 percent in Tunisia, from 16 to 6 percent in Algeria.[7]

Meanwhile, the population growth rates in Arab countries were exploding. Death rates were declining ahead of birth rates, and fertility rates, registering the number of children an average woman will have during her fertile years, remained extremely high. The population of all Arab countries increased from 55 million in 1930 to 90 million in 1960, and to 179 million in 1979.[8]

And therefore the rate of urbanization moved sharply upward. By the 1970s more than half the population in most Arab countries lived in cities, and larger and larger proportions of people lived in a few big cities. Baghdad grew from half a million in the 1940s to 1.5 million in the 1960s, to 3.8 million in the mid-1970s. Cairo, a city planned and built for 1.5 million, grew from 1.3 million in 1937, to 3.3 million in 1960, and then to 6.4 million in the mid-1970s. Saudi Arabia and Iraq had urban majorities too.[9] The desert and the fellah we associate with the Middle East were fading realities.

The new city populations came mostly from the declining countryside. Many also went abroad. There had always been work migration: Iranians had gone to Russia, Berbers from Algeria to France, people from Greater Syria to North and South America, and in the postwar period Turks had gone to Europe. Now the oil shock of 1973–74 boosted this labor migration to a huge new scale: in the early 1980s there were about 6 million Arab migrants, half in Saudi Arabia and the Gulf, the other half in Libya and Iraq. And another 4 million came to the Gulf from Asia, perhaps half from Muslim Pakistan.[10] But the oil economies could not accommodate all the people on the move in the Islamic world. Increasingly, they piled up in the shantytowns surrounding the old city centers, *bidonvilles* made of tin in Morocco and Algeria, *gourbivilles* made of peasant-style mud huts in Tunisia, *gecekondu*—housing built overnight—in Turkey. About a quarter of urban Turks lived in such places in 1981; 85 percent were from the countryside.[11] And so many were hard to employ: in Cairo in 1960, 7.5 percent of the workforce was employed in industry, 23 percent in services, and 66 percent, two-thirds of the total, constituted a huge floating population without fixed or regular work.[12]

These exploding populations were also getting younger (for that is what rising birthrates mean). By 1960 more than half the population in most countries was under twenty; by 1980 over 40 percent of the people in Muslim countries as a whole were under fifteen.[13] That meant, in turn, that education was not just part of the Arab socialist program: it was a massive challenge in almost every Islamic society. Many countries devoted serious effort and resources to education, and there were major advances. Literacy rose impressively in most places, to 60 percent in Syria; 50 percent in Algeria, Iran, Tunisia, and Qatar; and to over 40 percent in Egypt.[14] Students in all types of education in Egypt rose from under 2 million in 1953 to nearly 6 million, out of a population of nearly 40 million, in 1972.[15] The Middle East still had the lowest percentage of literate adults of any world region except South Asia, but the achievement was impressive nonetheless.[16]

The trouble was that, in social terms, education was top-heavy and had no correlation with the job market. Primary education was badly neglected compared to secondary schools and universities, which got the great bulk of policy attention and budget resources. In the Third World as a whole, 28.6 percent of students were in higher education; in the Arab world the figure was 34.3 percent. By the early 1980s Egyptian universities were pumping seventy-five thousand graduates *per year* into the job market, in an economy that was now starting to limp badly as the potential for state-led development began to shrink.[17]

Traditionally, a university education was the guarantee of a white-collar job, usually a state job, a decent standard of living, and a modicum of dignity. In the early 1960s Nasser's Egyptian state had made the contract formal by abolishing educational fees and making itself the employer of last resort for university graduates. In the early years of its expansion, the Egyptian state in fact hired graduates in large numbers, as did other states in the region. But the newly employed of the 1960s were going to be in place for decades, blocking entry for newer graduates. This meant that the latter would have to look for jobs more and more in the private economy. Beginning around 1970, the national states of the Islamic world in fact ceased to expand and began to turn more of the responsibility for growth over to the private sector. And the contraction came just at the time graduates needed the state most: by the mid-1980s, of a total population of around 270 million in the Middle East, most males had some education, and 15 to 25 million, or just under 10 percent, had secondary or university education.[18]

By around 1970, then, the Islamic world in its old Middle Eastern core had burgeoning cities that had ever younger populations and were producing ever more secondary school and university graduates, mostly males, who lived—whether at home or abroad—in settlements of deteriorating or rudimentary infrastructure, and with fewer and fewer prospects for jobs or dignity. Very many of these young men were from country families or families that had just moved from the country to small towns.[19] And if 25 million out of 270 million people are educated, the educated person lives more and more separated from the other 245 million people by that very education. The educated person needs to lead the others if the society is ever going to transcend the morass into which globalization has led it. But the educated person has no help: for the postcolonial state that had provided the education, and which had promised so much so soon, has proved inadequate, inept, incompetent, and corrupt.

EUROPE'S EAST AFTER 1870

Yet while the ingredients for political upheaval were specific to the Muslim world, they also were not wholly unique or new. In the half century between 1870 and the Bolshevik Revolution of 1917, many of the economic and social phenomena that marked the Islamic heartland a century later were also alive and well in the Russian and East European lands just to its north.

It was a time of considerable industrial growth. Between 1860 and 1910 industry's contribution to Russia's national income rose from 13 percent to 20 percent.[20] This was less than in the Islamic world a century later, but still impressive. Between 1870 and 1910 coal production rose from 693,000 tons to 36 million tons, oil production from 33,000 tons to 9.2 million tons.[21] Russian industrialization was also more broadly based, in the sense of being less dependent on the single commodity of oil, and therefore it provoked wider social changes, the growth of substantial working and middle classes. In Russia between 1860 and 1913, employment in mining and manufacturing, for instance, increased from 1.6 to 6.1 million, and it was famously concentrated in very large factories.[22]

Unlike the Islamic world a century later, Russia did not sacrifice its agricultural sector. By 1910 Russian agriculture was still employing 80 percent of the Russian workforce and supplying over half the national income. It was not doing well, but it was also not doing badly: the peasants at its base were consuming more and also supplying the growing cities with food.[23] Still, Russia too was living through a population explosion comparable to that of the Islamic world of the mid-twentieth century. If Arab populations increased from 55 to 179 million between the 1930s and the 1970s, Russia's went from 74 million in 1860 to about 170 million when World War I broke out in 1914.[24] And it did so for about the same reasons: a very high birth rate was maintained as death rates fell rapidly, while fertility rates also stayed high.

With an exploding population and fairly modest progress in both agriculture and industry, Russia too was a land of people on the move. Some went abroad: between 1909 and 1913 a little over 8 million Russian citizens left Russia every year, and a little *under* 8 million returned. And in this very large country, the 1897 census also showed that nearly 10 percent of all citizens lived outside their province of origin.[25]

So in Russia, too, urbanization was substantial. Between 1867 and 1897 the urban population of European Russia doubled to 12.5 million, and then over the next twenty years it doubled again, to nearly 26 million; thus it quadrupled in the half century before the revolution. As a proportion of the total population urban population rose from 10 percent in 1867 to 21 percent in 1916. Comparable to Cairo and Baghdad, St. Petersburg had expanded from about 500,000 in the 1860s to 2.2 million in 1914, Moscow from 350,000 to 1.7 million.[26]

Finally, Russia also had undergone great educational expansion. Between 1890 and 1913 school enrollment there rose from 2.2 to 7.6 million at the primary level, to over 500,000 in secondary schools and 130,000 in universities. This was not so large as little Egypt's half million in the 1970s, but it was big given the society's large peasant base and the caste-oriented government's (justi-fied) fear of educated outsiders. In Russia the emphasis was always on primary education, the inverse of the Islamic world's situation. Yet here too the achievement was real: in European Russia literacy rose from 22 per-cent to 33 percent between 1897 and 1920.[27]

An adult literacy percentage of one-third produced about the same effects in Russia then as adult literacy of two-fifths in Islamic societies half a century later. Russia had the same kinds of ingredients for turbulence: popu-lation pressure on growth, cities overwhelming their infrastructures, and increasing numbers of young people with secondary and higher education who faced uncer-tain prospects for jobs and dignity. And, in the most striking parallel of all, just as in the Islamic world of a generation ago, grievances in this Russian world were increasingly linked to the behavior of the *state*. In the Islamic world, by 1970 it was harder and harder to blame the departed colonizers for society's ills. In Russia, before the Emancipation of 1861, peasants had faced their land-lords; now they faced the state, and given the state's role in industrialization, they continued to face the state even when they had come to the city and become workers. So protest against employers and landowners translated more and more quickly into protest against the state.[28]

This was a recipe for the making of Raskolnikov, for Rodion Romanovich, Rodya, Fyodor Dostoyevsky's earnest, penniless student in *Crime and Punishment*, lying on his narrow bed in his shabby room in the Tsarist capital of St. Petersburg. Isolated, morally anguished, even tortured, he ends up killing an old woman with an ax to get her money. The setting is mid-century, the 1850s; but Raskolnikovs—the very name in Russian connotes "split" or "schism"—continued to appear generation after generation.

COMPARATIVE RADICALISMS

In the years that followed, the radicalism of these Russian intellectuals became more and more politicized, and the political radicalism of the Russian intelligentsia has a whole history of its own. The first great generation in the 1870s, called populist, the *narodniki*, went to the countryside to link up with the peasantry in order to lead it; the peasants turned them in to the authorities; and they turned to terror against senior officials. In 1881 they struck down the Tsar-Emancipator Alexander II. Over the next decade, savage state repression forced a confused search for other solutions, and by the 1890s those solutions included Marxism.[29] Marxism's position as the premier modernist ideology in Russia was consolidated only thereafter. But over time, radical opposition to the status quo became the norm for very large numbers of Russian intellectuals. Going abroad seemed not even to dent it: Lenin in Zurich or Trotsky in New York remained as resolutely radical as before their sojourns in the bosom of developing industrial capitalism. Marxists were on principle against terror as a political weapon; but they had many competitors, including social revolutionaries, who did *not* reject terror. So political killings became endemic in late imperial Russia. Governors, generals, bank presidents, police chiefs, archdukes all fell under Raskolnikov's ax, now festooned with political ribbons.

There were of course large differences between this Russia and the Islamic world around 1970. Critically, its industrialization was more broadly based than industrialization in Islam a century later. In particular, industrialization in Russia produced a growing working class whose concentration in large factories made it visible, and this helped to validate Marxism as the oppositional ideology of choice. Workers were also important in the politics of the modern Middle East.[30] Communists based in the new industrial complexes outside Cairo or in the Iranian oil fields could play serious political roles. But because industry in the Islamic world was so dispersed and so concentrated on oil, workers there were a much less powerful agent than they were in Russian politics. And it may be that the Russian peasants entering the factories were less attached to the old-time religion, in their case Russian Orthodox Christianity, than their Muslim counterparts a century later.

Neither Marxism nor Islamism reached its goal. In both late-nineteenth-century Russia and late-twentieth-century Muslim societies, the territorial state was the primary institution and engine of politics, dominant in almost all cases, smothering in many, always hard to resist and oppose. But for just that reason, both Russian and Islamic radicals adopted ideologies appealing to values that carried them above and beyond the territorial state, even when they could only be realized in practice by control of the territorial state.

As the twentieth century approached, for increasing numbers of Russian intellectuals that ideology was socialism. Their struggle was for a worldwide, classless society, in which exploitation of man by man would be abolished. Famously, Marx posited the eventual withering away of the state. But for Russian Marxists the objective was overwhelmingly to take over the Russian state in order to create socialist societies using state resources. Probably the Bolsheviks could have come to power only in the confusion and chaos produced in a shaky society by three hard years of World War I; the debate goes on. But of their intentions there was no doubt, and the rest of the twentieth century was spent dealing with some of the consequences.

For increasing numbers of Muslim intellectuals around 1970, on the other hand, the transcending ideology was the seventh-century utopia that had been part of Islam since (at least) its fourth decade: recreation of the community of Muslim believers, the *umma*, in the original purity and unity it had had under the Prophet and his companions. That utopia had some appeal to most Muslims, including scholars; but it usually had appealed most to the margins of the *umma*: to tribal pastoralists and the "little people" of the cities. But around 1970, postcolonial modernization was opening up an ideological vacuum in the new city populations it was producing.

The military catastrophe of the Six Days' War of 1967 was a body blow to Nasser's republican nationalism, his "Arab socialism." The kind of state-led development that Nasser promoted and others copied was running into the ground, exhausting its potential. And 1970, the year Nasser died, was also the year of Black September, when King Hussein of Jordan crushed a Palestinian uprising led by secularist intellectuals and drove them from his country. It was in the widening vacuum created by these failures that the perennial seventh-century utopia reemerged as the radical ideology of choice for Muslim intellectuals who felt more and more cornered by development and life.

The Egyptian Muslim Brotherhood, founded in 1928, was the grandfather of radical Islamist organizations. After its founder, Hasan al-Banna, was assassinated by the Egyptian authorities in 1949, his disciple Sayyid Qutb carried on as its chief postwar thinker. Sayyid Qutb was born into a family that had already moved to town; he also went abroad, to the United States, an experience that appears to have fired his radicalism. In this sense he was like Lenin or Trotsky. In 1964 Sayyid Qutb had published a brochure called *Signposts on the Path.*[31] *Signposts* became a kind of little green book for Islamist activists. In it Qutb rejected all forms of society except the "truly Islamic" one, the one that accepted only the sovereign authority of God, and that regarded the Qur'an as the source of all guidance for every aspect of human life.

> All other societies were societies of *jahiliyya* (ignorance of religious truth) . . . whether they were communist, capitalist, nationalist, based on other, false religions, or claimed to be Muslim but did not obey the *shari'a.* "The leadership of Western man in the human world is coming to an end . . . because the western order has played its part, and no longer possesses that stock of 'values' which gave it its predominance. . . . The scientific revolution has finished its role, as have 'nationalism' and the territorially limited communities which grew up in its age. . . . The turn of Islam has come."[32]

It is not quite clear that Sayyid Qutb was shifting the

terms of the competition when he claimed that previous Western strengths were simply being superseded, but "values" was certainly a realm where Muslims could feel superior. Still, it is also worth remarking that while this kind of confidence comes naturally to the ideologist, it is harder for the soldier of God who tries to act in accordance with the ideology. After 1917 Russian Marxism ruled an empire that spanned eleven time zones. Before that, however, it was a serious, authentic, but still marginal and hard-pressed movement. That is what radical Islamism has mainly been as well. Like the Bolsheviks before 1917, its adherents have in the main lived in quotidian darkness, bitterness, and only occasional exultation.

To strike a personal note, after the outrages of September 11, 2001, an academic friend who is a considerable expert on terrorism in late imperial Russia wrote to say that he found the perpetrators unfathomable, that he could not understand them. I urged him to read the biographies of the nineteen killers which had appeared in the *New York Times*, and then to go back to those of the young people in Russia he had studied, to understand how they became political assassins. He would find they had much the same life profiles, similar origins giving similar effects. And he called back to say they had: they were the same brand of people.

Excerpts from the document left behind by those who attacked the World Trade Center and the Pentagon are redolent not so much of confidence as of fear and desperate courage.

Remember: "How many small groups beat big groups by

the will of God." And his words, "If God gives you victory, no one can beat you". . . . Tighten your clothes, since this is the way of the pious generations after the Prophet. . . . Give us victory and make the ground shake under their feet. Pray for yourself and all of your brothers that they may be victorious and hit their targets and ask God to grant you martyrdom facing the enemy, not running away from it. . . . You should clench your teeth, as the pious early generations did. When the confrontation begins, strike like champions who do not want to go back to the world. Shout "Allahu Akbar . . . [God is great]."[33]

They were killers to be sure. But they were also uncertain young men, torn from their roots, belonging nowhere, at home only in their small groups, frightened, exalted. To understand them we can do worse than reread Dostoyevsky; we can do worse than contemplate Raskolnikov in his tiny room fingering his ax.

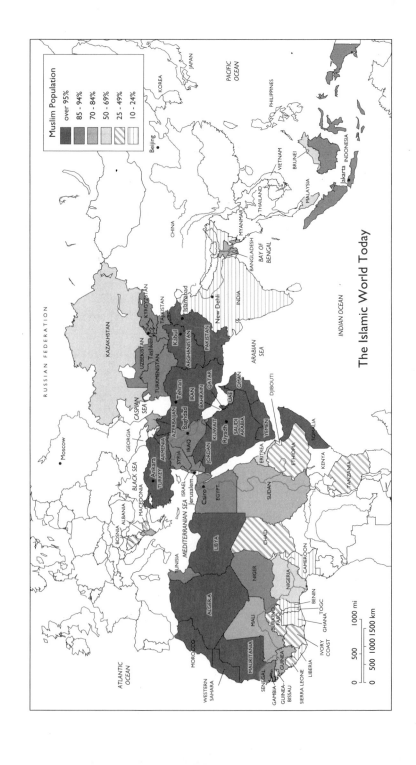

The Islamic World Today

Muslim Population

- over 95%
- 85 - 94%
- 70 - 84%
- 50 - 69%
- 25 - 49%
- 10 - 24%

ATLANTIC OCEAN

RUSSIAN FEDERATION

Moscow

PACIFIC OCEAN

Beijing

JAPAN

KOREA

CHINA

KAZAKHSTAN

BLACK SEA

CASPIAN SEA

GEORGIA

ARMENIA

AZERBAIJAN

TURKMENISTAN

UZBEKISTAN

Tashkent

KYRGYZSTAN

TAJIKISTAN

MACEDONIA

ALBANIA

BOSNIA

TURKEY

Ankara

SYRIA

IRAQ

Baghdad

Tehran

IRAN

Kabul

AFGHANISTAN

Islamabad

PAKISTAN

New Delhi

INDIA

MYANMAR

BANGLADESH

BAY OF BENGAL

VIETNAM

THAILAND

PHILIPPINES

BRUNEI

MALAYSIA

Jakarta

INDONESIA

MEDITERRANEAN SEA

ISRAEL

Jerusalem

Cairo

EGYPT

JORDAN

Riyadh

KUWAIT

BAHRAIN

QATAR

UAE

SAUDI ARABIA

OMAN

YEMEN

ARABIAN SEA

TUNISIA

LIBYA

ALGERIA

MOROCCO

WESTERN SAHARA

MAURITANIA

SENEGAL

GAMBIA

GUINEA BISSAU

GUINEA

SIERRA LEONE

LIBERIA

IVORY COAST

MALI

BURKINA FASO

GHANA

TOGO

BENIN

NIGER

NIGERIA

CAMEROON

CHAD

SUDAN

ERITREA

DJIBOUTI

ETHIOPIA

SOMALIA

KENYA

TANZANIA

INDIAN OCEAN

| 0 | 500 | 1000 mi |

| 0 | 500 | 1000 | 1500 km |

4

Political and Other Islams in IT-Led Globalization

Around 1970, the world and its Islamic component were on the verge of a new era. Globalization led and driven by coal, steel, and petroleum was giving way to globalization led and driven by information technology (IT). Year by year the premium was rising on mobility, openness, and transparency, and not only in the economy, but also in society and politics.

IT-led globalization has of course been a worldwide phenomenon, and it has naturally come first and been most pronounced in the technologically most advanced economies, where it has produced a slowly accelerating breakdown of old stabilities, including some that were not all that old. In the postwar era of big capital, big labor, and growing middle classes, politics in most Western countries was mainly "about" dividing up an expanding economic pie. Now these structures and the verities that had grown up around them began to dissolve; economies and societies were on the move again. Now, to compete for political leadership, it was increasingly necessary to build shifting coalitions issue by issue, and such coalitions could be built and maintained only on the basis of *values*.[1] This was a general phenomenon, but it included the reentry of religion into the political arena, up from the private sphere and back from the lumber room of history to which it had been consigned in the liberal era. Judaism and Christianity were among the religions involved; Islam was too.[2]

In the Islamic world, both the presiding postcolonial regimes and the emerging oppositions from the burgeoning younger generation now provided themselves with new technologies and equipment. Regimes adopted and tightened their control of television. From his exile in Paris, Ayatollah Khomeini's sermons and pronouncements against the Shah of Iran and the monarchy spread by audiocassette. And all sides in the swelling civil war among Muslims upgraded their armaments and reequipped themselves with better bombs and guns.

It is important to remember that this was a civil war mainly *among* Muslims. Many in the West thought the mounting violence was directed primarily at the Israelis and the Americans. Among the culminating events, after all, were the slaughter of Israeli athletes at the Munich Olympics in 1972, the American Embassy hostages in Tehran from 1979 to 1981, and the targeting of Americans in the takeover of the cruise ship *Achille Lauro* in 1985. Abu Nidal and Carlos the Jackal were as 1970s as bellbottoms and Afros. But the truth was that the main protagonists in this war *were* Muslims. That truth was sometimes masked because many of the protagonists were secularists, especially among Palestinians. Abu Nidal and Carlos were not particularly Islamic; they were mainly used by Muslim states against other states. But as it became harder and harder over the years to blame all the ills of the Islamic world on the now departed colonizers, whom Israel and the United States replaced only imperfectly, the gaze of the Islamic world's victims turned slowly but inexorably toward their *own* rulers. And those rulers were now Muslims.

At the outset there was room under most regimes, monarchies and republics alike, for both top-down modernizers—rulers seeking to adopt Western techniques in order to save the essentials—and adaptationists, the professionals and intellectuals who sought to shape Islam itself to the new Western values by which they were living. But both were badly battered in the first decades after independence. Perhaps they fared worst under republican nationalist regimes, with their state-led development, but the monarchies were often not much gentler. The large landowners who had supported anticolonial nationalism were practically destroyed by land reform. The professionals and intellectuals who had spearheaded adaptation were swamped by the rural exodus into the vastly expanded educational systems. And what capitalists remained, after the states had taken over economies and the foreigners among them had emigrated, were strapped to the chariot wheel of import-substitution industrialization. They became cronies almost by definition, producing in small protected markets to create rents for the state to spend on the ruling families, the army, and the bureaucracy.

The result was both a contraction and a curious reversal. Having shrunk and subordinated their civil societies, states increasingly hunkered down for support on their armies and police forces. And in anemic civil societies, the role of the erstwhile modernizers and adaptationists in resisting power was increasingly assumed by Islamists. So long as the enemy had been the colonial state, Islamists had remained on their traditional margins in the Islamic world. Now they came to the center, because they were proving in struggle that they were the most active and effective opponents of the inept and corrupt *post*colonial state.[3]

And now that politics were bipolar, states on one side and Islamists on the other, the war between them that broke out about 1970 was savage. The Iranian secret police of the Shah's last decade, the Savak, was savage; so was the victorious Islamic revolution after 1979, the executioners of Ayatollah Khalkhali's tribunals. In Egypt in 1981, Islamists finally assassinated Nasser's successor, Anwar as-Sadat, and they paid the price in the thousands. And when Hafez al-Assad's Syrian army retook the city of Hama from an insurrection of Sunni Islamists in 1982, the dead numbered in the tens of thousands.[4] In the 1990s government suppression of elections in Algeria that Islamists were sure to win triggered years of massacre, whole villages with their throats cut; here too the death toll reached the tens of thousands.[5]

But the contest was also a long and complex negotiation. For the regimes moved to Islamize themselves, precisely in order to coopt and isolate the Islamist enemy. In Jordan, King Hussein had always cultivated the local Muslim Brotherhood as a counterweight to Nasser. When he succeeded Nasser, Sadat started down the same path, calling himself the "believer-president." The media took to showing him in his *jallabiyya*, the long white garment associated with ordinary Muslims, doing Islamic things. Islamists killed him anyway, as "pharoah."[6] But over the decade such regime openings brought Islam into mainstream political discourse.

Muammar al-Qaddafi in Libya, Jafar al-Numayri in Sudan, the military dictator Zia al-Haq in Pakistan—all introduced extensive Islamization of laws and institutions. Programs like these were not always successful, not least because the leaders had a penchant for putting themselves above the *shari'a* they were purportedly introducing. In the end they were no more able to arrogate religious authority to themselves than the caliph al-Ma'mun had been in the eighth century. By the 1980s the Islamists whom Zia had brought into Pakistan's government were declaring martial law un-Islamic and joining the struggle for return to democracy.[7]

In one country, however, the struggle of radical Islamists with government ended in something new. That country was Iran. When Ayatollah Khomeini was in exile in Iraq before the revolution, he drew on Iran's Shi'i traditions, looked to its unique quasi-constituted *'ulama*, and set forth the concept of rule by the jurisconsult, either a single cleric or a group, the *velayat-e-faqih*. In the decade after the revolution this was then built into Iran's complicated constitutional structure. Not long before his death in 1989, Khomeini went further and ruled that in case of need the interest of the state and nation in fact takes priority over the *shari'a* itself. There could have been no clearer case of Islamism's function as the validator of the nation-state in the Islamic world. Probably Iran's special Shi'i character, reinforced during the brutal Iran-Iraq war of the 1980s, will make this salutary departure impossible to replicate elsewhere. But the case is at least proof that Islamic legitimation for the modern state *can* be found, and it has at least allowed Iran to weather the postcharismatic period with most democratic elements of its constitution intact and able to contest the undemocratic elements without large-scale violence.[8]

Then, too, this negotiation proved a two-way street. As the regimes Islamized, the Islamist radicals also made accommodations.[9] Some entered the national political systems of their countries. Since the late 1970s Islamic activist leaders have obtained cabinet positions not only in Iran and Pakistan, but also in Sudan, Jordan, Turkey, Kuwait, Yemen, and Malaysia. In most of these countries, and in Egypt too, Islamists were the leading opposition. Islamists participated in elections in Egypt, Algeria, Tunisia, Kuwait, and Yemen. They took 40 percent of the vote in Tunisian cities, 64 percent in Algiers, over 70 percent in Algeria's other towns. In Turkey they led a government until they were forced out by the military. Their entry into the system was tentative for both sides, highly back-and-forth, with no inevitability about it; but it was real.[10]

Other Islamists turned to community action rather than to politics on behalf of the faith. More and more of them decided that what was important was to affirm Islamic cultural identity rather than to seize or destroy power. For them, the locus of struggle shifted from the political arena to the family, the community, the school, the hospital. In Palestine the Muslim Brotherhood was so community-oriented that it splintered once the first *intifada* broke out in December 1987, with breakaway dissidents creating the more radical Hamas. Elsewhere too, for instance in Egypt, most Muslim Brothers operated carefully as community activists. In Pakistan, the largest Islamic organization is not a party at all but the Tablighi-Jama'at, a missionary organization that focuses (almost) entirely on reshaping of individual lives, on cultivating personal piety and right conduct.[11]

Of course, this turn from politics to community, from power to cultural identity, can cut a number of ways. First, it produces a huge new stress on form and conduct associated with Islam, on the ortho*praxy*, as distinguished from ortho*doxy*, which is so characteristic of Islam compared to other world religions. These new uplifters tended to see the center of gravity of public and private discourse in a fairly narrow range of *shari'a* law that emphasizes personal behavior and ritual. In the Subcontinent this is associated with the reformist Deoband school, dating back to the late nineteenth century. The Afghan Taliban trained in Deobandi *madrasseh* (religious training centers). Even compared to other Deobandis, they were extreme in their ritualistic rigor, their struggle against popular customs and ceremonies like pilgrimage to shrines, their hostility to Shi'ism, and their enforcement of female seclusion.[12] But the stress on ortho*praxy* inhabits the whole movement.[13]

Second, the shift from politics to community can give new salience to ethnicity. Historically, Islam has usually respected ethnicity even while trying to supersede it. And even modern Islamists work in practice within the framework of the territorial state that they wish to supersede in principle. But once cultural identity replaces political power as the main issue, it becomes more and more tempting to define that cultural identity in *ethnic* terms and make it the basis for *nationality*. Such a tendency, of course, runs counter to Islam's original globalizing impulse, but it is at work in the Islamic world today. For increasing numbers of Muslims, Islam functions first of all as a badge of ethno-national identity, distinguishing true citizens from false.[14] The phenomenon is not unknown elsewhere. Not so long ago Englishmen almost *had* to be Protestant and Poles *had* to be Roman Catholic. But in the Islamic world it gives an exclusivity to citizenship which is historically novel, and it can lead not only to sharper Sunni-Shi'a hostility, but also to self-consciously and explicitly anti-Jewish and anti-Christian activities on a scale that is also quite new, and very dangerous.[15]

Third and finally, the turn from Islamist politics to Islamic community action can also be tactical, a withdrawal from politics under pressure in order to lay or extend the basis for later, stronger reentry. That is certainly the nightmare of Egyptians who watch the spreading welfare activities of the Muslim Brotherhood and suddenly notice that private mosques outnumber state mosques, forty thousand compared to the six thousand under the Endowments Ministry.[16] It is the nightmare of Turks who see networks of Islamist schools and charities ready at any moment to morph into political infrastructure for whatever version of the Islamist party is currently operating. But by the 1980s global trends were starting to draw the world of Islam in rather different new directions.

These trends were of two kinds.

First, the Cold War was winding down. This made it

harder and harder for sitting Muslim regimes to extract rents from the Cold War protagonists in return for their support or acquiescence. Of course the Soviet side of the Cold War first shrank and then disappeared entirely at the turn of the 1990s. As "Political Communism" withered, the United States and its allies had less and less interest in paying high prices for the partnership of Muslim regimes, except in the Arab-Israeli context. And this was especially true when it came to dictatorships. What had been tolerated for the good of the cause during the Cold War was harder to tolerate once it wound down. In the 1990s, with communism gone, *democracy* became the global political flavor of the month almost *every* month, rather than every once in a while. So political liberalization, democratization, and civil society became the dominant themes of Muslim political discourse.[17]

Second, accelerating IT-led globalization fit into and gave urgency to that discourse, for it tended to leave the old Islamic heartland area, and especially its republican nationalist regimes, high and dry when it came to economic partnership with the engines of the global economy.[18] The Third World debt crisis that broke upon the world in 1982 triggered a new package of prescriptions of how economies could best achieve competitiveness and growth. This was the so-called "Washington consensus," the main components of which were liberalization, deregulation, elimination of government subsidies, privatization, open international trade, and export-led growth. The 1990s then added a stress on institutions, rule of law, and consolidating openness and transparency. And the emergence of this new consensus put almost all the regimes of the Middle East and North

Africa at a huge new disadvantage. Almost all of them, after all, republics and monarchies alike, use the state to allocate and distribute economic rents in order to maintain the extensive patronage networks that keep them in power. None is interested mainly in economic growth per se; all are information-shy.

Two-thirds of this Islamic core area's total exports are in mineral fuels. Since 1983 OPEC has been unable to control the price of oil because it cannot control its members' output; between 1981 and 1998 oil revenues to Arab OPEC countries and Iran fell from $250 billion a year to $110 billion in constant dollars. There was volatility too: in just one year, between 1997 and 1998, Saudi oil revenues fell by half, overall revenues by 31 percent. Prices rose somewhat in 2002, in the wake of September 11 and anticipation of an American attack on Iraq, but they were unlikely ever to recover their earlier buoyancy so long as Russia, which had overtaken Saudi Arabia as the world's largest producer, kept supporting price stability.[19] With economic policy attention shifting to the private sector and with the Cold War over, most forms of official assistance and foreign aid also shriveled away in the 1990s: from a high of 30 percent of world development assistance in 1977, the region's share dropped to 17 percent in 1990 and 9 percent in 1997. The new private flows of foreign direct investment that were replacing aid worldwide then passed the region by: the Middle East share of FDI to developing countries (if Turkey is excluded) fell from 11.6 percent in 1990 to 3.3 percent in 1997 and 4.3 percent in 1998.

Meanwhile, the socioeconomic features mentioned in the last chapter have remained in place. Population continues to explode. For twenty-two Arab countries, it grew from less than 200 million in 1980 to 280 million in 2000, and is expected to reach between 410 and 459 million in 2020.[20] Egypt, Turkey, and Iran all approached or passed the 70 million mark at century's end; Pakistan was near 140 million. Iran's population had doubled since the revolution. According to the U.S. Census Bureau, well over half the populations of Egypt, Syria, Saudi Arabia, Iran, and Iraq were under twenty years old; in Pakistan the figure was 61 percent, in Afghanistan 62 percent.[21] The core regions are now urbanized: in 1996 the urban population as a percentage of the total stood at over 90 percent in Kuwait and Qatar; over 80 percent in Lebanon and Saudi Arabia; over 70 percent in Bahrain, Iraq, and Jordan; over 60 percent in Turkey and Iran; over 50 percent in Tunisia and Syria; and over 40 percent in Morocco and Egypt.[22] Unemployment in the Middle East region averaged 15 percent; in poor performers like Algeria it afflicts half the labor force.[23]

State sectors remain huge. In Egypt, total government employment accounts for about a third of the labor force; the state employs more than half of all workers with postsecondary education. In Iran the state and the foundations run by the clergy control four-fifths of the economy, employ about a fifth of the labor force, and handle three-quarters of all imports. In Saudi Arabia, the royal family collects and redistributes the national revenue, to its allied Najdi commercial families and to itself: of $7 billion in windfall oil revenues that bubbled up in 1999, $4 billion went to its own members. But regime after regime faces the task of staying in power with declining resources. And since their economies do not attract outside investors, there are few alternative resources waiting in the wings.[24]

So a squeeze is underway, responses to which naturally have been varied. But the *main* response has been a series of tentative, partial attempts at adaptation. It resembles the "defensive modernization" of the nineteenth century, say of the Ottomans or Egyptians, and so far it has had the same partial and contradictory effects. Efforts are made to reform individual sectors, and instead of the synergy that can be created by reform across a broad front, the result is tension between sectors. In politics, participation is opened up—after the Gulf War even the Saudis tried a consultative assembly, and have managed to increase its standing since then—but in many places then closes down again. Reform starts and stops and starts again as fear of the political consequences (of starting *or* stopping) clutches regimes by the throat. When Algeria's republican nationalist regime abolished elections in January 1992, rather than submit to the certain electoral victory of the Islamic Salvation Front, the FIS, it was not atypical. Since Iranian President Khatami's election in 1997 the country has been in a kind of Brownian political movement, urgent activity leading nowhere in particular. In Turkey the military forced out the country's first Islamist prime minister and banned his Refah or Welfare Party. In King Hussein's last years in Jordan, in Mubarak's Egypt, the late 1990s witnessed *de*liberalization, a squeeze-down rather than an expansion of reform.[25]

But early in the new millennium, when everything is ostensibly "Islamic" again, in some places elements of a new kind of synthesis are emerging. Not only are Islamists participating in government, formally or de facto, but they are slowly building the financial bases they need to participate confidently and responsibly. Those bases have always been there in Turkey, with the small and medium provincial capitalists in the Anatolian heartland who had remained culturally Islamic and resent the state's favors to its big-business cronies. Early in the twenty-first century, it is growing in other countries too. So-called Islamic finance, with profit-sharing arrangements in place of classic interest, is spreading. It accounts for 5 percent of deposits in Egypt, and could have more without state efforts to restrict it. There the Sheikh of Al-Ahzar University issues *fatwa*s (legal opinions) against it; he is of course paid by the government. And despite their formal Islamism, the Saudi rulers forbid it *entirely* because they want control of everything.[26]

It also turns out that in terms of economic policy not only Refah in Turkey but the FIS in Algeria were enthusiastic free marketeers. Their opponents, of course, claimed this was merely tactical, that if and when they come to power they too would want rents to maintain the networks needed to keep them in power, and would use the state to extract them. But it is also true that, just because they focus on *cultural identity* rather than state power, the strong sensitivity to economic and social injustice many Islamists feel is perfectly compatible with substantial indifference to the specific forms the economy should take, so long as Islamic identity can be preserved. The Taliban were an extreme example during their time in Afghanistan: fixated on dress, appearance, and ritual, they could not have cared less about the economy. But the same fine indifference to system marks Islamists everywhere; and it could make them better stewards of adjustment to IT-led globalization than the statist regimes currently in place.[27]

The same holds for political systems. By the 1990s many Islamists were enthusiastic democrats: Refah and FIS once again come to mind. In these cases, too, opponents say their avowed enthusiasm is only a way to protect themselves in opposition until they gain power. But, as in economics, Islamists may well have fewer theoretical allergies to democracy than many of the hardshell Muslim republicans they oppose, not to speak of the monarchists.[28] With reference to the Subcontinent, Barbara Metcalf has speculated that Deobandi indifference to political and economic systems has the effect in practice of making religion a matter of personal private life, separate from politics, even if they are indivisible in theory.[29] This is happening elsewhere as well, a phenomenon that could produce an Islamically legitimated version of the separation of sacred and profane, of "church" and state, which many Westerners continue to insist is uniquely Western, a product of the Renaissance and Reformation whose equivalents Islam famously has never had.

Furthermore, theory followed practice: in the Islamic discourse of the 1990s, the wind was in the sails of those who were finding Islamic bases for democracy, pluralism, and civil society. Just as eighteenth-century scholars proclaimed that every Muslim had the right and duty to exercise *ijtihad*, now the Sudanese Islamist Hasan al-Turabi argued that every Muslim is an *'alim*, a member of the *'ulama*. The familiar Islamic concepts of consultation, assent, selection of leaders, and consensus are now being given democratic content. Figures like Hasan Hanafi in Egypt, Abdul-Karim Soroush in Iran, and Rashid Ghannoushi in Tunisia are permitted, restricted, repressed, permitted again; but they carry on, and they have more and more resonance.[30]

There will still be problems. The dispersion of religious authority in Islam will remain a problem. To strike a personal note again, while still a U.S. diplomat in 1998 I complained to Taliban leader Mullah Rabbani about Osama bin Laden's *fatwa* of February of that year making it a religious obligation to kill Americans, and his reply was that Osama was not a scholar and therefore could not issue *fatwa*s. When I rejoined that the *fatwa* could still get Americans killed, Mullah Rabbani waved away the point.[31] This dispersion will always tempt states to substitute for the cohesion that does not exist in the religion, and pious Muslims will then resist. The struggle will go on.

But meanwhile the radical Islamists in the style of the 1970s, of the devoted readers of Sayyid Qutb and Maulana Maududi, of the killers of Sadat, were increasingly isolated and on the run. Osama bin Laden and the veterans of the old Islamist wars he gathered around him are of that breed; but in the end they could find no place in settled Muslim societies. Driven to Sudan, deprived of his Saudi citizenship, Osama was then driven from Sudan to ruined Afghanistan, where he was protected by those peculiar Taliban, with their different but also extreme brand of Islamism; and that meant he was doubly protected, since there were enough Islamists within the Pakistan state to protect the Taliban in turn.

Such Islamists will continue to reproduce, because the

conditions that gave them life are still there. They are increasingly high-tech and global; their interest in or loyalty to any state is disappearing; they exist only for themselves and their radical dream of recreating the seventh century.[32] Defining everything in terms of religion, these globalist radicals attack not only Shi'a but now Jews and Christians as such. Such people in Karachi, Pakistan, made the journalist Danny Pearl tell the camera that his mother was a Jew, his father was a Jew, he was a Jew; it is almost certainly such people who gunned down a Shi'i doctor in Karachi and attacked Christians in Islamabad in March 2002. They constantly expand and elevate their targets. Osama started as the enemy of the Soviet presence in Afghanistan, then became the enemy of the American presence in his native Saudi Arabia, and then he discovered the starving children of Iraq, the martyred women of Palestine, as the Twin Towers began to cast their baleful shadow.[33]

That, however, is not a sign of *confidence*; it is a sign of desperation. People like Osama are fewer. Before the Twin Towers the number of *world* terrorist incidents had been on a declining trend for years, from the record 484 in 1991 to 298 in 1995, and then up again at the end of the decade: 392 in 1999, 423 in 2000. CIA figures showed deaths from terrorism down from 4,833 in the decade of the 1980s to 2,587 in the 1990s.[34] September 11 and its aftermath drove the figures up to start the new decade. But except for the aberrant attack on the tourists at Luxor in 1997, there was no serious incident in Egypt in the half decade that followed.

Islamist killers were still out there. In December 1995 the Egyptian Embassy down the street from the American Embassy in Islamabad was blown up by an Egyptian radical outfit called Gamaa Islamiyya. But Gamaa members are generally younger than their predecessors, drawn now from villages as well as cities, more radical.[35]

And they were also on the run: the Gamaa struck in Islamabad because it had become so hard to strike in Egypt itself. The fighters for Osama who left behind the pathetic papers described in the *New York Times* had the same profile. Of thirty-nine recruits of Kashmir-oriented Harakat ul-Mujahadin, all were unmarried, many were under twenty, few had gone beyond secondary school. "Knows how to make sweets," it says of one; "knows how to embroider," of another. "Cleanliness; clean beds and tents once a week," their rules say; "do not leave compound; no political discussions; no arguments; no drugs; go to bed early."[36] It is heartbreaking.

They and others like them will continue to conspire, to work in the back rooms of overcrowded cities under the shadow of the police. They will wreak damage and take lives. But there are fewer and fewer places where they can operate with the space and security Osama had in Afghanistan.[37] There is now *no* other place where they can have the double layer of protection, like Russian nesting dolls, that Osama had there. And there is a dwindling number of ruined places that can provide even a single layer: the southern Philippines, northern Sumatra, Somalia, perhaps Yemen. And all of these are on coasts within easy reach of American power.[38]

Of course such societies are also complex; of course various outcomes are possible.[39] Of course military power will not be enough. Americans and their allies will need to deal with the conditions that produce such people as well as the people themselves.[40] For that, Americans and their allies will need to mobilize resources, to understand the real nature of the challenges, to muster the political will to apply resources to those challenges on a sustained basis. September 11 sparked a new debate in this country about American resources and American responsibilities in world affairs, and that debate needs to keep going in the right directions. Understanding, I think, is one key; this book's purpose has been to help citizens to delineate the challenges for themselves, to understand how specific and real those challenges are, but also how limited they are.

Livable outcomes will not depend only or even mainly on Americans: they will depend mainly on Muslims. Muslims now number over a billion on our common planet; they are a sixth of our common humanity. Their religion and their experience give them almost the full spectrum of the possibilities of which humanity is capable. The Islamic accomplishment, the creativity and good will of Muslims, are treasures for all mankind.

Today's challenges to our Muslim brothers and sisters and their children are very great. Their economies, societies, and polities are under huge structural pressures from IT-led globalization in post–Cold War circumstances. But the opportunities are very great as well. It may now be possible to break free at last from the truncations and prevarications that were forced on Muslims and invented by Muslims in conditions of Western encroachment and domination. It may now be possible to break the linkage of modernity with Western domination that has afflicted the Islamic world for nearly two centuries. It may now be possible at last for Muslims to shape for themselves a modernity that is consonant with Islamic belief and Islamic authenticity. It may now be possible, at last, for countries besides Iran to give the nation-state the kind of *Islamic* legitimacy it has always had trouble developing. With that kind of legitimacy, the nation-state can give Muslims the vehicle for prosperity, personal freedom, and identity it once was in the West and can still be for much of the rest of the world.

Islam gives Muslims fully sufficient resources for new and more successful syntheses of what is modern and what is theirs. There is nothing inevitable about those syntheses; and the effort to reach them will certainly be punctuated by catastrophes even without the special incubus of the Israeli-Palestinian conflict. But such syntheses of what is modern and what is Islamic are possible and achievable. And surely it is the Americans—the Americans who are still the Western world's most religious people, who are citizens of a nation that was founded on values and is necessarily held together by values—surely it is the Americans who are in the *best* position to understand and support the efforts of Muslims to fashion new and better lives for themselves *and* for us in this new phase of our life together on earth.

Bibliographical Essay

The literature on Islam in history is vast, and this makes any selection from it necessarily arbitrary. What follows is basically a choice of works that have been most useful to me in preparing this book. They are cited in rough chronological order, from Islam's beginning to today. Some are the high points in a lifetime of reading; others were particularly helpful in my effort to capture recent and contemporary trends. I have stressed the most recent sources, on the assumption that wisdom, like knowledge, is somehow cumulative; but since that is of course a frail assumption, older works are cited too. Assuming most readers will be fluent in English, I have limited myself to works available in that language, at least in translation. More specific data (also from English-language sources) are cited in the endnotes. Much work of value is still left out. But taken together these readings have permitted me to develop whatever comprehensive view emerges in this book, and they should permit others to develop views of their own.

There are many good straightforward short introduc-

tions to Islam in history. Among the best are Karen
Armstrong, *Islam: A Short History* (New York: Modern
Library, 2002); Malise Ruthven, *Islam: A Very Short
Introduction* (Oxford: Oxford University Press, 2000),
and *Islam in the World*, 2nd ed. (Oxford University
Press, 2000), 2–121; and John L. Esposito, *Islam: The
Straight Path*, 3rd ed. (New York: Oxford University
Press, 1998), 1–114. Annemarie Schimmel, *Islam: An
Introduction* (Albany: State University of New York
Press, 1992), is perhaps most attentive to the cultural and
especially mystical aspects. Older, but still useful despite
its lamentable title, is H. A. R. Gibb, *Mohammedanism:
An Historical Survey* (1953; reprint, London: Oxford Uni-
versity Press, 1981). On a broader register, I have drawn
much over the past quarter century on Marshall G. S.
Hodgson, *The Venture of Islam* (Chicago: University of
Chicago Press, 1974). Published posthumously in three
volumes, it is a monument of modern scholarship.
While controversial like everyone else, when stacked up
against some other great students of "civilizations"
Hodgson emerges as the least derivative (and Eurocen-
tric): Paul B. Rich, "Civilisations in European and
World History: A Reappraisal of the Ideas of Arnold
Toynbee, Fernand Braudel, and Marshall Hodgson,"
European Legacy 7, no. 3 (June 2002): 331–42. Another
but shorter monument to liberal scholarship is Albert
Habib Hourani, *A History of the Arab Peoples* (Cam-
bridge, Mass.: Belknap Press of Harvard University
Press, 1991) (Harvard intended to publish a new edition,
with Malise Ruthven as coauthor, in February 2003).
But for a good, vehement short critique of Western
scholarship, including Gibb's, readers seeking an "anti-

Orientalist" perspective (as they also should) may enjoy
Hisham Sharabi, "The Scholarly Point of View: Politics,
Perspectives, Paradigm," in Hisham Sharabi, ed., *Theory,
Politics, and the Arab World: Critical Responses* (London:
Routledge, 1990), 1–51.

The tribal element has been distinctively crucial in
Islamic history, and while (or because) tribalism has
shrunk drastically in most Islamic societies over the last
century, its importance in the Islamic experience continues to be vigorously debated. The classic analysis is one
of the great works of world sociology and politics, from
the fourteenth century C.E.: Ibn Khaldun, *The Muqaddimah*, trans. Franz Rosenthal, 2nd ed. (Princeton, N.J.:
Princeton University Press, 1967). There is a convenient
one-volume abridgment in paper, edited by N. J.
Dawood: *The Muqaddimah: An Introduction to History*
(Princeton, N.J.: Bollingen Series, Princeton University
Press, 1967). For recent commentary, see Philip S.
Khoury and Joseph Kostiner, eds., *Tribes and State Formation in the Middle East* (London: I. B. Tauris, 1991),
especially Ira M. Lapidus, "Tribes and State Formation
in Islamic History," 25–47, and Ernest Gellner, "Tribalism and the State in the Middle East," 108–26.

My views on Islam's first three centuries have been
decisively shaped by H. A. R. Gibb's (unpublished) lectures on the period at Harvard in 1958–59, and of course
by Marshall Hodgson's *The Classical Age of Islam*, volume 1 of *The Venture of Islam*. But the relation of "religion" and "politics" has always been special in Islam (as
with all great religions), and since both modern Islamists
and their Orientalist critics in the West like to claim that
in Islam they are "inherently" and inextricably welded

together, if not identical, the relationship(s) of Islam and the state have been a lively special problem. Here my best guides have been Albert Hourani, "The Islamic State," in his *Arabic Thought in the Liberal Age* (London: Oxford University Press, 1962), 1–24; and Ira M. Lapidus, "State and Religion in Islamic Societies," *Past and Present*, no. 151 (May 1996): 3–27.

For the era of political dissolution and religious expansion and renewal between the tenth and sixteenth centuries of the Common Era, I have relied on Hodgson's *The Expansion of Islam in the Middle Periods*, volume 2 of *The Venture of Islam*, but supplemented by the first half of Ira M. Lapidus, *A History of Islamic Societies*, 2nd ed. (Cambridge: Cambridge University Press, 2002). There are also incisive views on the Sunni revival and the new synthesis in Fazlur Rahman's (unfinished) *Revival and Reform in Islam: A Study of Islamic Fundamentalism*, ed. Ebrahim Moosa (Oxford: Oxford University Press, 2000).

The coexistence of a strong "private" realm and a weak or tyrannical state that emerged during this "middle" period as a feature of very many Islamic societies makes "society" a kind of third term in the debate over Islam and the state. Here the classic works are Ira M. Lapidus, *Muslim Cities in the Later Middle Ages* (1967; reprint, Cambridge: Cambridge University Press, 1984); Richard W. Bulliet, *The Patricians of Nishapur: A Study in Medieval Islamic Social History* (Cambridge, Mass.: Harvard University Press, 1972); and Roy J. Mottahedeh, *Loyalty and Leadership in an Early Islamic Society*, 2nd ed. (London: I. B. Tauris, 2001). Mottahedeh's review of Bulliet in *Journal of the American Oriental*

Society 95, no. 3 (July–September 1975): 491–95, is also useful.

The balance of inertia and innovation in Islamic thought and practice beginning in this period has also inspired lively and continuing controversy. This is partly because modern Islamic reformists of all stripes must necessarily raise the banner of *ijtihad*, rightful effort to apply revealed truth to unforeseen situations. The best contemporary scholarship on these issues is in Wael B. Hallaq, *A History of Islamic Legal Theories* (Cambridge: Cambridge University Press, 1997), and his *Authority, Continuity, and Change in Islamic Law* (Cambridge: Cambridge University Press, 2001). For a judicious short summary, see his "Ijtihad," in John L. Esposito, ed., *The Oxford Encyclopedia of the Modern Islamic World* (New York: Oxford University Press, 1995), 2: 178–81.

Once again, Hodgson has been my main mentor on the early modern empires and their new syntheses: *The Gunpowder Empires and Modern Times*, volume 3 of *The Venture of Islam*. Again, however, I have supplemented him with (the second half of) Lapidus's *History of Islamic Societies*.

I have called the eighteenth century C.E. a "silver age" for the Islamic world, a time of intellectual and spiritual renewal while political authority was dispersing downward from its now habitual centers, but before the Western impact became a major determinant. The key works for intellectual and religious life are the first half of John O. Voll, *Islam, Continuity, and Change in the Modern World*, 2nd ed. (Syracuse, N.Y.: Syracuse University Press, 1994); and Ahmad Dallal, "The Origins and Objectives of Islamic Revivalist Thought, 1750–1850,"

Journal of the American Oriental Society 113, no. 3 (July–September 1993): 341–59. There are also interesting insights in a collection of conference papers edited by Nehemia Levtzion and John O. Voll, *Eighteenth-Century Renewal and Reform in Islam* (Syracuse, N.Y.: Syracuse University Press, 1987). Economic and social developments in the Middle East for the whole modern period, including these years, are now captured succinctly but with penetrating analysis in Joel Beinin, *Workers and Peasants in the Modern Middle East* (Cambridge: Cambridge University Press, 2001). The pioneering work on how intellectual and socioeconomic change were related is still Peter Gran, *Islamic Roots of Capitalism: Egypt, 1760–1840* (Austin: University of Texas Press, 1979). H. A. R. Gibb and Harold Bowen, *Islamic Society and the West*, volume 1, *Islamic Society in the Eighteenth Century* (London: Oxford University Press, 1965), was pioneering in its day but has been largely overtaken by subsequent scholarship. (No further volumes were published.)

Beinin and the second half of Voll's *Islam, Continuity, and Change* have also been important sources for my understanding of the century and a half of Western domination beginning in the early nineteenth century. But also essential for this whole period is Reinhard Schulze, *A Modern History of the Islamic World* (London: I. B. Tauris, 2000). The literature on the relation(s) between Islam and modernity is extensive, and it is naturally proliferating further since September 11, 2001. Some high points are cited in relation to the text, but I have found two works of particular interest conceptually: Sami Zubaida, *Islam, the People, and the State* (London: I. B. Tauris, 1993); and Roxanne L. Euben, *Enemy in the Mirror: Islamic Fundamentalism and the Limits of Modern Rationalism* (Princeton, N.J.: Princeton University Press, 1999). For the most prominent Muslim thinkers wrestling with the dilemmas of Islamic modernization, Charles Kurzman has now given us an extremely useful sourcebook, *Modernist Islam, 1840–1940* (Oxford: Oxford University Press, 2002), and there are good, succinct accounts and analyses not only in Fazlur Rahman and Esposito's *Islam: The Straight Path*, but also in John L. Esposito, *Islam and Politics*, 4th ed. (Syracuse, N.Y.: Syracuse University Press, 1998); and the late Nazih N. Ayubi, *Political Islam: Religion and Politics in the Arab World* (London: Routledge, 1991).

My third chapter spotlights the comparable socioeconomic origins of radical socialism in Europe in the late nineteenth century and the radical Islamism of our own times, and specific elements are documented in the endnotes. In terms of that limited comparison, the works I have found most valuable on the Islamic side, besides Beinin, have been Alan Richards and John Waterbury, *A Political Economy of the Middle East: State, Class, and Economic Development* (Boulder, Colo.: Westview Press, 1990); and, conceptually, Terry Lynn Karl, *The Paradox of Plenty: Oil Booms and Petro-States* (Berkeley: University of California Press, 1997).

In general, however, comparisons between today's Islamism(s) and earlier radicalism(s) have not been much pursued by scholars. Some of those sparked by September 11 are referred to in the text, and there is an earlier one, inspired by the fall of communism, that sets a standard for depth and richness in a small compass: Ernest Gellner, "Islam and Marxism: Some Comparisons," *International Affairs* 67, no. 1 (1991): 1–6. However, the shock of September 11 widened many lenses, and once scholars are better able to see Islam as part of the world, the situation may improve.

We are somewhat better served for the "Islamist era" that began around 1970 and for the complex "something else" that is superseding it, as globalization driven by information technology supersedes globalization based on manufacturing, on "blood and iron." For starters, we have a stimulating recent effort by Charles S. Maier to define the elements of the changeover on a worldwide scale: "Consigning the Twentieth Century to History: Alternative Narratives for the Modern Era," *American Historical Review* 105, no. 3 (June 2000): 807–31. But there are also dozens of examinations of the new stage of globalization. One among several that are particularly relevant to the Islamic landscape is Peter L. Berger and Samuel P. Huntington, eds., *Many Globalizations: Cultural Diversity in the Contemporary World* (Oxford University Press, 2002). Two decades earlier, a decade before the Cold War ended, Jürgen Habermas had already laid the theoretical base for the new focus on cultural rather than political conflict, in "New Social Movements," *Telos*, no. 49 (Fall 1981). In between there is a whole literature; there is much to choose from.

On the political side, the second half of Reinhard Schulze's *Modern History* and John Esposito's *Islam and Politics* are useful synthetic treatments, especially when supplemented by Roger Owen, *State, Power, and Politics in the Making of the Modern Middle East*, 2nd ed. (London: Routledge, 2000). There are readable accounts of the "Islamist era" itself by two Frenchmen who argue strongly (and controversially) that it is over: Olivier Roy, *The Failure of Political Islam* (Cambridge, Mass.: Harvard University Press, 1994); and Gilles Kepel, *Jihad: The Trail of Political Islam* (Cambridge, Mass.: Belknap Press of Harvard University Press, 2002). But the essays on individual Islamic societies and countries in Martin E. Marty and R. Scott Appleby, eds., *Fundamentalisms Observed* (Chicago: University of Chicago Press, 1991), also remain extremely valuable.

The "post-Islamist era" is closer to us in time, and it is controversial both conceptually and politically, especially after September 11. Hence its record is still scattered and debated in scores of books and hundreds of articles. A number are cited in the endnotes; the following have provided me with more general insights.

Some of the key economic underpinnings of the changeover are on display in Clement M. Henry and Robert Springborg, *Globalization and the Politics of Development in the Middle East* (Cambridge: Cambridge University Press, 2001); and Jahangir Amuzegar, *Managing the Oil Wealth: OPEC's Windfalls and Pitfalls* (London: I. B. Tauris, 1999). There is also a useful reminder that similar challenges can inspire varying responses, in Kiren Aziz Chaudhry, *The Price of Wealth: Economics and Institutions in the Middle East* (Ithaca, N.Y.: Cornell University Press, 1997).

On the political side, there are a number of texts aspiring to synthetic overviews. Those most useful (and plausible) to me have been Barbara Metcalf, "Islam in Contemporary Southeast Asia," in Robert W. Hefner and Patricia Horvatich, eds., *Islam in an Era of Nation-States: Politics and Religious Renewal in Muslim Southeast Asia* (Honolulu: University of Hawaii Press, 1997), 309–20; Metcalf's "'Traditional' Islamic Activism: Deoband, Tablighis, and Talibs," *Social Science Research Council Essays*, http://www.ssrc.org/sept11/essays/metcalf.htm, 1–8; and Olivier Roy's "Neo-Fundamentalism" in the same SSRC collection (. . . essays/roy.htm). There is however also good material on the "overt" modernizers: Charles Kurzman, ed., *Liberal Islam: A Sourcebook* (New York: Oxford University Press, 1998); John L. Esposito and John O. Voll, *Makers of Contemporary Islam* (Oxford: Oxford University Press, 2001); and (by two of them), Nilüfer Göle, "Islam in Public: New Visibilities and New Imaginaries," *Public Culture* 14, no. 1 (Winter 2002): 173–90; and Abdelwahab Meddeb, "Islam and Its Discontent: An Interview with Frank Berberich," *October*, no. 99 (Winter 2002): 3–20. And John Esposito's latest published texts are always worth a read: at this point (January 2003) they are *Unholy War: Terror in the Name of Islam* (Oxford: Oxford University Press, 2002), and now (an even more popular) *What Everyone Needs to Know About Islam* (Oxford: Oxford University Press, 2002).

By and large, however, it is too soon to ask for histories of Islam today: the Owl of Minerva has not yet spread its wings. Once it does, it is my hope that this short study will find a place beneath them.

Notes

Chapter 1: The First Thousand Years

1. Ian Buruma and Avishai Margalit, "Occidentalism," *New York Review of Books* 49, no. 1 (January 17, 2002): 4–7. The contemporary phase of the debate began with Edward W. Said, *Orientalism* (New York: Pantheon Books, 1978).

2. But see also examples of Western scholars who accept today's Islamist definitions of what Islam "is": Daniel Pipes, *In the Path of God: Islam and Political Power* (New York: Basic Books, 1983); and Samuel P. Huntington's remarks in "Islam in the 21st Century," *New Perspectives Quarterly* 19, no. 1 (Winter 2002): 6: "Pluralism (in the West) has been empowered (since the Early Modern religious wars) by a division between religion and politics unknown in the Islamic world. This merger of political and religious life generates conflict." For a judicious and accessible intermediate approach, see Richard W. Bulliet, "The Crisis Within Islam," *Wilson Quarterly* (Winter 2002): 11–19.

3. In addition to the Lapidus and Gellner pieces cited in the Bibliographical Essay (Ira M. Lapidus, "Tribes and State Formation in Islamic History," and Ernest Gellner, "Tribalism and the State in the Middle East," in Philip S. Khoury and Joseph

Kostiner, eds., *Tribes and State Formation in the Middle East* [London: I. B. Tauris, 1991], 25–47, 108–26), see Anthony Black, *The History of Islamic Political Thought: From the Prophet to the Present* (New York: Routledge, 2001), 350 ff.; and Stanley Kurtz, "Root Causes," review of *What Went Wrong?* by Bernard Lewis, *Policy Review*, no. 112 (April–May 2002): 73–81. On their continuing (if limited) relevance, see Neil MacFarquhar, "In Iraq's Tribes, U.S. Faces a Formidable Wild Card," *New York Times*, January 5, 2003.

4. On Eastern India, see the detailed study by Richard Maxwell Eaton, *The Rise of Islam and the Bengal Frontier, 1204–1760* (Berkeley: University of California Press, 1993).

5. Cited in Albert Habib Hourani, *Arabic Thought in the Liberal Age* (London: Oxford University Press, 1962), 14.

6. *Ijtihad* was certainly alive and well in the practice of medieval Tlemcen in Morocco: Osama Abi-Mershed, "Degrees of Interpretive Autonomy: *Ijtihad* and the Constraints of Competence and Context in Late Medieval Tilimsan," *Islam and Muslim-Christian Relations* 13, no. 1 (January 2002): 25–48. And for the medieval pedigree of other reformist terms, see John O. Voll, "Renewal and Reform in Islamic History: *Tajdid* and *Islah*," in John L. Esposito, ed., *Voices of Resurgent Islam* (New York: Oxford University Press, 1983), 32–47. But the pressure to conform to opinions reached through *ijma'* was heavy, and increased with time.

7. The phrase is Samuel P. Huntington's: see *The Clash of Civilizations and the Remaking of World Order* (New York: Simon and Schuster, 1996), 254, and *passim*. He argues that the phenomenon is as old as Islam and "flows from the nature of the two religions and the civilizations based on them" (210), rather than from specific circumstances like the Byzantine-Ottoman struggle. Contemporary Islamists are hence among the most avid and convinced adherents of his thesis: cf. Khaled Ahmed, "Huntington's 'Application' of Clash of Civilisations (*sic*) Hypothesis to India," *Friday Times* (Lahore), April 24–30,

1998, 9; and "Afghan Islamic Leader Says the War of Civilizations Has Begun," an interview with Gulbuddin Hekmatyar, in *Al-Hayat* (London), November 2, 2002, translated and posted on http://www.afgha.com, November 7, 2002.

8. For a vivid new view of how Mongol habits stayed with Moghul ruling families, now see Ruby Lal, "The 'Domestic World' of Peripatetic Kings: Babur and Humayun, c. 1494–1556," *Medieval History Journal* 4, no. 1 (January–June 2001): 43–82.

Chapter 2: Globalization by Blood and Iron

1. On the gradual thickening of ties with the West, see Professor Joel Beinin's genial summary of the 1740–1839 period, *Workers and Peasants in the Modern Middle East* (Cambridge: Cambridge University Press, 2001), 21–43.

2. John O. Voll argues for this view in the first part of *Islam, Continuity, and Change in the Modern World*, 2nd ed. (Syracuse, N.Y.: Syracuse University Press, 1994), cited in the Bibliographical Essay.

3. So argued by Ahmad Dallal, in "The Origins and Objectives of Islamic Revivalist Thought, 1750–1850," *Journal of the American Oriental Society* 113, no. 3 (July–September 1993): 341–59, cited in the Bibliographical Essay, with its fine brief analyses of Shah Wali Ullah (1703–62), Muhammad ibn 'Abd al-Wahhab (1703–87), 'Uthman ibn Fudi (1754–1817), and Muhammad 'Ali al-Sanusi (1787–1859). The Muslims of the Subcontinent have continued to have a history of their own, and the story is now carried forward toward our own day by Ayesha Jalal, *Self and Sovereignty: Individual and Community in South Asian Islam Since 1850* (London: Routledge, 2000).

4. For a striking example, the Yemeni-Egyptian conservative reformist Muhammad 'Ali al-Shawkani (d. 1832), see L. Clarke, "The Shi'i Construction of *Taqlid*," *Journal of Islamic Studies* 12, no. 1 (2001): 40–64.

5. For an accessible brief account of Naqshbandiyya reformism, see Malise Ruthven, *Islam in the World*, 2nd ed. (Oxford University Press, 2000), 268–81. Shah Wali Ullah was a Naqshbandiyya sheikh.

6. Peter Gran's *Islamic Roots of Capitalism: Egypt, 1760–1840* (Austin: University of Texas Press, 1979), cited in the Bibliographical Essay, is fundamental on this topic. Timur Kuran has also written extensively on the relation(s) of Islam and economics in this period; see his "Islam and Underdevelopment: An Old Puzzle Revisited," *Journal of Institutional and Theoretical Economics* 53, no. 1 (March 1997): 41–71, and "The Islamic Commercial Crisis: Institutional Roots of Economic Underdevelopment in the Middle East," *Journal of Economic History* 63, no. 2 (forthcoming, June 2003).

7. In addition to Dallal, there are short accounts of Ibn 'Abd al-Wahhab and Wahhabism in most basic treatments; for example, Ruthven, *Islam in the World*, 265–68.

8. For the top-down modernizers and the adaptationists, cf. John O. Voll, *Islam, Continuity, and Change in the Modern World*, 2nd ed. (Syracuse, N.Y.: Syracuse University Press, 1994); Joel Beinin, *Workers and Peasants in the Modern Middle East* (Cambridge: Cambridge University Press, 2001); and also Albert Habib Hourani, *A History of the Arab Peoples* (Cambridge, Mass.: Belknap Press of Harvard University Press, 1991).

9. For an intriguing scholarly comparison between the calls-to-arms of the nineteenth-century Sudanese Mahdi Muhammad Ahmed (1882) and Osama bin Laden (1998), see Malise Ruthven, "The Eleventh of September and the Sudanese Mahdiya in the Context of Ibn Khaldun's Theory of Islamic History," *International Affairs* 78, no. 2 (April 2002): 339–51.

10. For an earlier instance in India, see Gail Minault, *The Khilafat Movement* (New York: Columbia University Press, 1982); for today, Ahmed Rashid, "The Hizb ut-Tahrir: Reviving

the Caliphate," in his *Jihad: The Rise of Militant Islam in Central Asia* (New Haven, Conn.: Yale University Press, 2002), 115–36.

11. Quoted phrase from Beinin, *Workers and Peasants*, 108.

12. Islam's relationships to modernity are of course extremely complex, and have given rise to a growing literature. For these issues I have relied on Voll and Beinin, and also Reinhard Schulze, *A Modern History of the Islamic World* (London: I. B. Tauris, 2000), cited in the Bibliographical Essay; but I have also found the following useful: Ernest Gellner, *Muslim Society* (Cambridge: Cambridge University Press, 1981); Masoud Kamali, "Civil Society and Islam: A Sociological Perspective," *Archives européennes de sociologie* 42, no. 3 (2001): 457–82; Dale F. Eickelman and Armando Salvatore, "The Public Sphere and Muslim Societies," *Archives européennes de sociologie* 43, no. 1 (2002): 92–115; Juan R. I. Cole and Denis Kandiyati, "Nationalism and the Colonial Legacy in the Middle East and Central Asia: Introduction," *International Journal of Middle East Studies* 34, no. 2 (May 2002): 189–203; and Saad Eddin Ibrahim, "Civil Society and Prospects of Democratization in the Arab World" (1995), in his *Egypt, Islam, and Democracy: Critical Essays*, with a new postscript written in Tora Farm Prison in 2001 (Cairo: American University in Cairo Press, 2002), 245–67. At sixty-three and in poor health, Ibrahim was sentenced in July 2002 to seven years' prison, and in August the U.S. government responded to public pressure by withholding certain aid monies from Egypt: Thomas L. Friedman, "Bush's Shame," *New York Times*, August 4, 2002; "On Trial in Egypt," *Boston Globe*, August 11, 2002; and Dan Ephron, "US, Tying Rights Case to Aid, Irks Egyptians," *Boston Sunday Globe*, September 8, 2002.

13. Beinin, *Workers and Peasants*, 96.

14. This is very much Schulze's point: see *A Modern History*, 33.

15. Sami Zubaida has been the most eloquent spokesperson

for this view, and for the nation-*creating* role of the state in the Middle East as elsewhere: see *Islam, the People, and the State* (London: I. B. Tauris, 1993), cited in the Bibliographical Essay, but also "Is Iran an Islamic State?" in Joel Beinin and Joe Stork, eds., *Political Islam* (London: I. B. Tauris, 1997), 103–19; and Zubaida, "The Fragments Imagine the Nation: The Case of Iraq," *International Journal of Middle East Studies* 34, no. 2 (May 2002): 205–15.

16. Roxanne L. Euben relates the two developments and modern Islamic radicalism in *Enemy in the Mirror: Islamic Fundamentalism and the Limits of Modern Rationalism* (Princeton, N.J.: Princeton University Press, 1999). See also Fred R. Dallmayr's review in *International Studies Review* 3, no. 1 (Spring 2001): 171–74; and Euben's "Contingent Borders, Syncretic Perspectives: Globalization, Political Theory, and Islamizing Knowledge," *International Studies Review* 4, no. 1 (Spring 2002): 23–48.

17. There are convenient summaries of these intellectuals' lives and thought in John L. Esposito, *Islam: The Straight Path*, 3rd ed. (New York: Oxford University Press, 1998), 115–57, and in his *Islam and Politics*, 4th ed. (Syracuse, N.Y.: Syracuse University Press, 1998), 48–78. We can hear their voices in Charles Kurzman, ed., *Modernist Islam, 1840–1940: A Sourcebook* (Oxford: Oxford University Press, 2002).

18. Kurzman, *Modernist Islam*, 99–156; but also Nazih N. Ayubi, "Political Islam: Intellectual Sources," in his *Political Islam: Religion and Politics in the Arab World* (London: Routledge, 1991), 120–57, cited in the Bibliographical Essay.

19. Schulze, *A Modern History*, 112–92, is an excellent guide to this whole period.

20. On Egypt, see Saad Eddin Ibrahim, "Egypt's Landed Bourgeoisie (1994)," reprinted in his *Egypt, Islam, and Democracy*, 109–34.

21. Terry Lynn Karl, *The Paradox of Plenty: Oil Booms and*

Petro-states (Berkeley: University of California Press, 1997), cited in the Bibliographical Essay. For a recent if somewhat foreshortened view of the interplay of oil and democratic prospects in the region, see Thomas L. Friedman, "Drilling for Freedom," *New York Times*, October 20, 2002.

Chapter 3: Comparative Radicalisms

* "The crime I committed is horrible, and it was premeditated. I therefore deserve the death sentence, gentlemen of the jury. But even if I were less guilty, I see before me men for whom my youth inspires no pity, and who wish through me to punish and discourage forever a whole class of young people: born in low circumstances, more or less oppressed by poverty, but fortunate enough to have acquired a good education and the audacity to mix in what the pride of the rich calls society." [My translation.]

1. The penalties of backwardness are powerfully described for Eastern Europe in Iván T. Berend and György Ránki, *The European Periphery and Industrialization, 1870–1914* (Cambridge: Cambridge University Press, 1982), and, at greater length, in their *East Central Europe in the 19th and 20*th Centuries (Budapest: Akadémiai Kiadó, 1977).

2. There are a number of useful recent reflections comparing and contrasting today's Islamisms with earlier radicalisms, albeit from different angles than mine. For an overview, see Alan Richards, "At War with Utopian Fanatics," *Middle East Policy* 8, no. 4 (December 2001): 5–9. Late-nineteenth-century European anarchism provides interesting parallels in John O. Voll, "Bin Laden and the New Age of Global Terrorism," *Middle East Policy* 8, no. 4 (December 2001): 1–5; and for the international community's response, in Richard Bach Jensen, "The United States, International Policing, and the War Against Anarchist Terrorism," *Terrorism and Political Violence* 13, no. 1 (Spring 2001): 15–46. Communism is the reference for Mark N. Katz, "Osama bin Laden as Transnational Revolutionary

Leader," *Current History* 101, no. 652 (February 2002): 81–85; and Amitai Etzioni, "Opening Islam," *Society* 39, no. 5 (July–August 2002): 29–35. Both are somewhat taxonomic, and perhaps the antidote lies in art: Tom Stoppard's trilogy of plays on nineteenth-century Russian radicals, "The Coast of Utopia," opened in London in the fall of 2002; cf. Adam Cohen, "Three Plays, Nine Hours Celebrating Political Imperfection," *New York Times*, October 22, 2002: "The new world that was ushered in on Sept. 11, 2001, is an old world in one respect: political utopianism, with all its blood-soaked passion, is back." The most stimulating brief substantive parallels are still in Ernest Gellner's older remarks cited in the Bibliographical Essay: "Islam and Marxism: Some Comparisons," *International Affairs* 67, no. 1 (1991): 1–6. There Gellner suggests that Western dominion led to the triumph of Islam's "high" form— "the urban-based, strict, unitarian, nomocratic, puritan and scripturalist Islam"—over the "lower"—ecstatic, ritualistic, unpuritanical, and rustic—along with its tribal social base, and that this in turn has permitted Islam's unique modernization on its own terms, without secularization.

3. Recounted briefly in Joel Beinin, *Workers and Peasants in the Modern Middle East* (Cambridge: Cambridge University Press, 2001), 114–41; and at greater length in Alan Richards and John Waterbury, *A Political Economy of the Middle East: State, Class, and Economic Development* (Boulder, Colo.: Westview Press, 1990), cited in the Bibliographical Essay.

4. Figures are from Elias H. Tuma, *Economic and Political Change in the Middle East* (Palo Alto, Calif.: Pacific Books, 1987), 133.

5. Ibid.

6. Once again, see Terry Lynn Karl, *The Paradox of Plenty: Oil Booms and Petro-states* (Berkeley: University of California Press, 1997), *passim*.

7. From Tuma, *Economic and Political Change*, 109; but see also Richards and Waterbury, *Political Economy*, 143–71.

8. Figures are from Albert Habib Hourani, *A History of the Arab Peoples* (Cambridge, Mass.: Belknap Press of Harvard University Press, 1991), 437.

9. Figures are from ibid., 438, and Richards and Waterbury, *Political Economy*, 94.

10. Background and figures are from Georges Sabagh, ed., *The Modern Economic and Social History of the Middle East in Its World Context* (Cambridge: Cambridge University Press, 1989), 29–38.

11. Richards and Waterbury, *Political Economy*, 266–76. On three Istanbul *gecekondu* in the late 1960s and early 1970s, before Islamist ascendancy, see Kemal H. Karpat, *The Gecekondu: Rural Migration and Urbanization* (Cambridge: Cambridge University Press, 1976).

12. Figures are from Hourani, *Arab Peoples*, 386.

13. From ibid., 373; and Richards and Waterbury, *Political Economy*, 91–95.

14. From Richards and Waterbury, *Political Economy*, 114, and *passim*; and Sabagh, *Modern Economic and Social History*, 140.

15. Roger Owen, *State, Power, and Politics in the Making of the Modern Middle East*, 2nd ed. (London: Routledge, 2000), 30.

16. Richards and Waterbury, *Political Economy*, 114.

17. Ibid., 119, 125.

18. Ibid., 110, 119.

19. The *locus classicus*, based on 1977 interviews with imprisoned Islamist radicals, is still Saad Eddin Ibrahim, "Anatomy of Egypt's Militant Islamic Groups: Methodological Notes and Preliminary Findings," *International Journal of Middle East Studies* 12 (1980): 423–53, also available in Ibrahim, *Egypt, Islam, and Democracy: Critical Essays* (Cairo: American Univer-

sity in Cairo Press, 2002), 1–34. But Beinin notes that already in 1914 the protagonist of M. Husayn Haikal's classic novel *Zaynab* was also a newly educated village boy, like Stendhal's Julien Sorel, only now politicized (in his case as a nationalist): Beinin, *Workers and Peasants*, 75.

20. Berend and Ránki, *European Periphery*, 159.

21. Arcadius Kahan, *Russian Economic History: The Nineteenth Century* (Chicago: University of Chicago Press, 1989), 69.

22. Employment figures from Peter Gatrell, *The Tsarist Economy, 1850–1917* (London: B. T. Batsford, 1986), 84–85; see also M. E. Falkus, *The Industrialization of Russia, 1700–1914* (London: Macmillan, 1972), 68, 83.

23. Gatrell, *Tsarist Economy*, 139–40.

24. Kahan, *Russian Economic History*, 71.

25. Gatrell, *Tsarist Economy*, 63, 69.

26. Ibid., 67.

27. Figures are from Kahan, *Russian Economic History*, 171–75.

28. See Gatrell, *Tsarist Economy*, 233.

29. Norman M. Naimark is the chronicler of this transition: *Terrorists and Social Democrats: The Russian Revolutionary Movement under Alexander III* (Cambridge, Mass.: Harvard University Press, 1983).

30. Beinin's *Workers and Peasants* documents their role in Arab countries.

31. There is a vast literature on the Muslim Brotherhood, Hasan al-Banna, and Sayyid Qutb. For recent works, see Yvonne Hazbeck Haddad and John L. Esposito, *The Islamic Revival Since 1988: A Critical Survey and Bibliography* (Westport, Conn.: Greenwood Press, 1997). For an accessible short account, see John L. Esposito, *Islam and Politics*, 4th ed. (Syra-

cuse, N.Y.: Syracuse University Press, 1998), 131–48; for close analysis, see Ibrahim M. Abu-Rabi, *Intellectual Origins of Islamic Resurgence in the Modern Arab World* (Albany: State University of New York Press, 1996), which also treats Hizbollah mentor Muhammad Husayn Fadlallah. For a vivid recent update, see Jeffrey Goldberg, "In the Party of God," *New Yorker*, October 14 and 21, 2002, 180–95.

32. Cited in Hourani, *Arab Peoples*, 445–46.

33. Cited in *New York Times*, September 29, 2001.

Chapter 4: Political and Other Islams

1. Jürgen Habermas was of course the pioneer analyst of this shift: "New conflicts (in society) no longer arise in areas of material reproduction. . . . Rather, the new conflicts arise in areas of cultural production, social integration and socialization. . . . In short, the new conflicts are not sparked by *problems of distribution*, but concern *the grammar of forms of life*": "New Social Movements," *Telos*, no. 49 (Fall 1981): 33. But see also my remarks at a mid-1987 conference: "Technology and Public Policy in East-West Relations," in F. Stephen Larrabee, ed., *Technology and Change in East-West Relations* (New York: Institute for East-West Security Studies, 1988), 199–206.

2. There is a good primer on "fundamentalisms" of all kinds in R. Scott Appleby, "Fundamentalism's Many Faces," *Foreign Policy* (January–February 2002): 16–23. The shift in focus within Islam from politics to cultural identity was already discernible to scholars by the mid-1980s, for example, in P. J. Vatikiotis, *Islam and the State* (London: Croom Helm, 1987), 48. By the new millennium there were whole dense books on the interrelationships, for example, Tibi Bassam, *Islam Between Culture and Politics* (Basingstoke, Eng.: Palgrave, 2001). Many will still prefer to see this cultural focus as "essential" to Islam defined as a "non-Western" phenomenon. But for an intermediate view from one of the founding fathers of this school,

chastened by years of discussion, see Peter L. Berger, "The Cultural Dynamics of Globalization," introduction to Peter L. Berger and Samuel P. Huntington, eds., *Many Globalizations: Cultural Diversity in the Contemporary World* (Oxford University Press: 2002), 1–16. Berger writes that "Islamic movements in Turkey and all over the Muslim world clearly intend an alternative modernity. . . . [They are] seeking to construct a modern society that participates economically and politically in the global system but is animated by a self-consciously Islamic culture" (13).

3. These processes can be conveniently followed in the second half of Reinhard Schulze, *A Modern History of the Islamic World* (London: I. B. Tauris, 2000), and, on the political side, in the first half of Roger Owen, *State, Power, and Politics in the Making of the Modern Middle East*, 2nd ed. (London: Routledge, 2000). See also Saad Eddin Ibrahim, "Civil Society and Prospects of Democratization in the Arab World" (1995), now available in *Egypt, Islam, and Democracy: Critical Essays* (Cairo: American University in Cairo Press, 2002), 245–67; Clement M. Henry and Robert Springborg, *Globalization and the Politics of Development in the Middle East* (Cambridge: Cambridge University Press, 2001), 163; and Abdelwahab Meddeb, "Islam and Its Discontents: An Interview with Frank Berberich," *October*, no. 99 (Winter 2002): 3–20.

4. Malise Ruthven, "The Eleventh of September and the Sudanese Mahdiya in the Context of Ibn Khaldun's Theory of Islamic History," *International Affairs* 78, no. 2 (April 2002): 339–51, soberly puts it at ten thousand, that is, over three times the dead of September 11.

5. Among hundreds of accounts of this "Islamist era," Gilles Kepel, *Jihad: The Trail of Political Islam* (Cambridge, Mass.: Belknap Press of Harvard University Press, 2002), is recent and accessible. Kepel is the second of two eloquent Frenchmen who argue that the era is basically over; the other is Olivier Roy, *The Failure of Political Islam* (Cambridge, Mass.: Harvard Univer-

sity Press, 1994). Both have many critics. For examples, see Charles E. Butterworth on Roy (and Mohammed Arkoun's *Rethinking Islam* [1994]), in Charles E. Butterworth and I. William Zartman, eds., *Between the State and Islam* (Cambridge and Washington, D.C.: Cambridge University Press and the Wilson Center, 2001), 14–30; and Mohammed Hocina Benkleira on Kepel, in *Studia Islamica*, no. 92 (2001): 211–14. For a convenient recent retrospective, cf. Guilain Denoeux, "The Forgotten Swamp: Navigating Political Islam," *Middle East Policy* 9, no. 2 (June 2002): 56–81.

6. John L. Esposito, *Islam and Politics*, 4th ed. (Syracuse, N.Y.: Syracuse University Press, 1998), 236–38. On varieties of Sufi revival in the wreckage of Egyptian nationalism after 1967, see Michael Gilsenan, "The World Turned Inside Out: Forms of Islam in Egypt," in his *Recognizing Islam: Religion and Society in the Modern Middle East*, 2nd ed. (London: Croom Helm, 1990), 215–50.

7. Gilsenan, "World Turned Inside Out," 163–70 (Qaddafi), 171–86 (Zia), 265–70 (Numayri).

8. The literature on the Iranian Revolution and the years since is properly vast and varied. For a convenient short account into the 1990s, see Sandra Mackey, *The Iranians: Persia, Islam, and the Soul of a Nation* (New York: Penguin Putnam, 1998), 211–380. On Khomeini's January 1988 pronouncement and his role as legitimizer of the temporal state, see, in addition to Mackey (340): Sami Zubaida, "Is Iran an Islamic State?" in Joel Beinin and Joe Stork, eds., *Political Islam* (London: I. B. Tauris, 1997), 107; Baqer Moin, *Khomeini: Life of the Ayatollah* (London: I. B. Tauris, 1999), 294; Anthony Black, *The History of Islamic Political Thought: From the Prophet to the Present* (New York: Routledge, 2001), 335–36; Daniel Brumberg, *Reinventing Khomeini: The Struggle for Reform in Iran* (Chicago: University of Chicago Press, 2001), 135; and David Menashri, *Post-Revolutionary Politics in Iran: Religion, Society, and Power* (London: Frank Cass, 2001), 13–46. Vanessa Martin's

Creating an Islamic State: Khomeini and the Making of a New Iran (London: I. B. Tauris, 2000) is excellent, but basically ends in 1979–80.

9. This "negotiation" is particularly well documented for non-Arab Muslim countries. For Southeast Asia, see Jason F. Isaacson and Colin Rubinstein, *Islam in Asia* (New Brunswick, N.J.: Transaction, 2002); Manning Nash, "Islamic Resurgence in Malaysia and Indonesia," in Martin E. Marty and R. Scott Appleby, eds., *Fundamentalisms Observed* (Chicago: University of Chicago Press, 1991), 715–24; and Robert W. Hefner, *Civil Islam: Muslims and Democratization in Indonesia* (Princeton, N.J.: Princeton University Press, 2000), which takes the story through late 1999, when Abdurrahman Wahid was elected president. Donald J. Porter, "Citizen Participation Through Mobilization and the Rise of Political Islam in Indonesia," *Pacific Review* 15, no. 2 (2002): 201–24, carries it past September 11, and his *Managing Politics and Islam in Indonesia* (London: Routledge, 2002) makes it comprehensive. For Pakistan, see S. V. R. Nasr's groundbreaking "Islamic Opposition in the Political Process: Lessons from Pakistan," in John L. Esposito, ed., *Political Islam: Revolution, Radicalism, or Reform?* (Boulder, Colo.: Lynne Rienner, 1997), 179–207. For Turkey, see David Shankland, *Islam and Society in Turkey* (Huntington, Eng.: Eothen Press, 1999); and Marvine Howe, *Turkey Today: A Nation Divided over Islam's Revival* (Boulder, Colo.: Westview Press, 2000). For poor Afghanistan and its contrary direction, see Barnett Rubin, *The Fragmentation of Afghanistan: State Formation and Collapse in the International System* (New Haven, Conn.: Yale University Press, 1995); and Ahmed Rashid, *Taliban: Militant Islam, Oil, and Fundamentalism in Central Asia* (New Haven, Conn.: Yale University Press, 2000). For Central Asia, see Deniz Kandiyati, "Post-Colonialism Compared: Potentials and Limitations in the Middle East and Central Asia," with good references, *International Journal of Middle East Studies* 34, no. 2 (May 2002): 279–97.

10. Figures are from Esposito, *Islam and Politics*, 301, 306,

319. Other useful accounts from the Arab world during the hopeful heights of negotiation in the mid-1990s: Timothy D. Sisk, *Islam and Democracy: Religion, Politics, and Power in the Middle East* (Washington, D.C.: United States Institute of Peace, 1992); Rex Brynen, Baghat Koremy, and Paul Noble, *Political Liberalization and Democratization in the Arab World*, vol. 1, *Theoretical Perspectives* (Boulder, Colo.: Lynne Rienner, 1995), vol. 2, *Comparative Experiences* (Boulder, Colo.: Lynne Rienner, 1998); Abdo Baaklini, Guilain Denoeux, and Robert Springborg, *Legislative Politics in the Arab World: The Resurgence of Democratic Institutions* (Boulder, Colo.: Lynne Rienner, 1999). For the Palestinians, see Barry Rubin, *The Transformation of Palestinian Politics: From Revolution to State-Building* (Cambridge: Cambridge University Press, 1999). For a convenient chronology on Algeria, see Yahia H. Zoubir, "Algeria: Islamic Secularism and Political Islam," in Rolin G. Mainuddin, ed., *Religion and Politics in the Developing World: Explosive Interactions* (Aldershot, Eng.: Ashgate, 2002), 78–101. And for a comparable contemporary "negotiation" between another "religion" and another political system, Christophe Jaffrelot, *The Hindu Nationalist Movement in India* (New York: Columbia University Press, 1996). For 2002, see Amy Waldman, "Hindu Nationalists Win Landslide Vote in Indian State," *New York Times*, December 16, 2002.

11. To borrow a phrase from the Russian populist movement of the 1870s, this brand of community activism is "going to the people" (mainly in the cities), and since it is now more than two decades old, it is beginning to find its chroniclers and commentators. Cf. Asif Bayat, "Activism and Social Development in the Middle East," *International Journal of Middle East Studies* 34, no. 1 (February 2002): 1–28, with an extensive bibliography; Barbara Metcalf, "'Traditional' Islamic Activism: Deoband, Tablighis, and Talibs," *Social Science Research Council Essays*, http://www.ssrc.org/sept11/essays/metcalf.htm, 1–8; and Olivier Roy's "Neo-Fundamentalism," in the same SSRC collection (. . . essays/roy.htm); both of the latter are cited in

the Bibliographical Essay. Roy here pursues a phenomenon he was one of the first to identify, in *Failure of Political Islam*, 75–88. Roy points out that lowering the focus from the universal to the local draws Islamists willy-nilly toward the national, since states define the local environment, and he sees the struggle of mainstream Islamist movements shifting toward "a kind of Islamo-nationalism." On Hamas, see Shaul Mishal and Avraham Sela, *The Palestinian Hamas: Vision, Violence, and Coexistence* (New York: Columbia University Press, 2000). For more on Tablighi-Jama'at, see Mumtaz Ahmad, "Islamic Fundamentalism in South Asia: The Jamaat-i-Islami and the Tablighi Jamaat of South Asia," in Marty and Appleby, *Fundamentalisms Observed*, 457–530. For fresh and fascinating individual insights into how it works concretely, see Salwa Ismail, "The Popular Movement Dimensions of Contemporary Militant Islam: Socio-Spatial Determinants in the Cairo Urban Setting," *Comparative Studies in Society and History* 42, no. 2 (April 2000): 363–93; Alev Çinar, "National History as a Contested Site: The Conquest of Istanbul and Islamist Negotiation of the Nation," *Comparative Studies in Society and History* 43, no. 2 (April 2001): 364–91; Christopher Houston, "The Brewing of Islamist Modernity: Tea Gardens and Public Space in Istanbul," *Theory, Culture, and Society* 18, no. 6 (December 2001): 77–98; and Ergun Özbudun and E. Fuat Keyman, "Cultural Globalization in Turkey: Actors, Discourses, Strategies," in Berger and Huntington, *Many Globalizations*, 296–321, with citations. Nilüfer Göle has some stimulating general reflections on the phenomenon: "Islam in Public: New Visibilities and New Imaginaries," *Public Culture* 14, no. 1 (Winter 2002): 173–90, also cited in the Bibliographical Essay.

12. Metcalf, "Islamic Activism," *passim*.

13. For a related *fait divers*, see James Dao, "Detainees Stage Protest at Base (Guantánamo) over a Turban," *New York Times*, March 1, 2002. The keepers gave in.

14. Cf. especially Barbara Metcalf, "Islam in Contemporary

Southeast Asia," in Robert W. Hefner and Patricia Horvatich, eds., *Islam in an Era of Nation-States: Politics and Religious Renewal in Muslim Southeast Asia* (Honolulu: University of Hawaii Press, 1997), 309–20; and Juan R. I. Cole and Deniz Kandiyati, "Nationalism and the Colonial Legacy in the Middle East and Central Asia: Introduction," *International Journal of Middle East Studies* 34, no. 2 (May 2002): 197.

15. For example, David Rohde, "Gunmen Kill 6 at a Christian School in Pakistan," *New York Times*, August 6, 2002; "Raid on Christian Hospital in Pakistan Raises Fears of New Surge of Militancy," *New York Times*, August 10, 2002; and "Gunmen Kill 7 Workers for Christian Charity in Pakistan," *New York Times*, September 26, 2002. See also Susan Sachs, "With Missionaries Spreading, Muslims' Anger Is Following," *New York Times*, December 31, 2002; and "Defending France's Jews," *New York Times* editorial, January 16, 2003.

16. Esposito, *Islam and Politics*, 246.

17. On this discourse, cf. Charles Kurzman, ed., *Liberal Islam: A Sourcebook* (New York: Oxford University Press, 1998); and more recently and briefly, John L. Esposito, *Unholy War: Terror in the Name of Islam* (Oxford: Oxford University Press, 2002), 133–51. For a march-past of Muslim liberals before and after September 11, there is a whole issue on "Islam in the 21st Century" in *New Perspectives Quarterly* 19, no. 1 (Winter 2002).

18. Unless otherwise specified, figures and themes for what follows are drawn from Henry and Springborg, *Globalization, passim*, which is thoroughly researched and elegantly argued.

19. Cf. Neela Banerjee, "Stable Oil Prices Are Likely to Become a War Casualty, Experts Say," *New York Times*, October 2, 2002; and Leon Aron, "Russian Oil and U.S. Security," *New York Times*, May 5, 2002.

20. Executive summary of the UN Development Program's *Arab Human Development Report 2002*, cited at http://www.undp.org/ahdr, released July 2, 2002, 2. See also Ginijesh Pant,

"Islamic Resurgence and Neoliberal Economic Reforms in West Asia," *International Studies* (New Delhi) 38, no. 4 (October–December 2001): 323–40. According to the UN Population Fund's "State of World Population 2002," released December 7, 2002, Iran's 2002 population was 72.4 million and was projected to rise to 121.4 million by 2050: http://www.unfpa.org.

21. Elaine Sciolino, "Radicalism: Is the Devil in the Demographics?" *New York Times*, December 9, 2001.

22. Bayat, "Activism and Social Development," 25n.

23. Henry and Springborg, *Globalization*, 59.

24. Another devastating picture of appalling mismanagement, as well as the constraints, can be found in Jahangir Amuzegar, *Managing the Oil Wealth: OPEC's Windfalls and Pitfalls* (London: I. B. Tauris, 1999). Key indicators are updated by a group of Arab intellectuals in a fresh self-critique, the UNDP *Arab Development Report 2002, passim*. See Barbara Crossette, "Study Warns of Stagnation in Arab Societies," *New York Times*, July 2, 2002; Thomas L. Friedman, "Arabs at the Crossroads," *New York Times*, July 3, 2002; and "An Arab Call to Action," *New York Times* editorial, July 4, 2002. However, similar causes need not have similar effects, since countries respond differently: cf. Pete W. Moore, "Rentier Fiscal Crisis and Regime Stability in the Middle East: Business and State in the Gulf," *Studies in Comparative International Development* 37, no. 1 (Spring 2002): 34–56; and especially Kiren Aziz Chaudhry, *The Price of Wealth: Economics and Institutions in the Middle East* (Ithaca, N.Y.: Cornell University Press, 1997) (cited in the Bibliographical Essay), on Saudi Arabia and Yemen, driven toward less and more representation respectively; this work is dense but destined to be a classic.

25. On the start-stop-start path of reform, see Richard Augustus Norton, ed., *Civil Society in the Middle East* (Leiden: E. J. Brill, 1995); Daniel Brumberg, "Islamists and the Politics of Consensus," *Journal of Democracy* 13, no. 3 (July 2002):

109–15; and Adrian Karatnycky's balance sheet, "Muslim Countries and the Democracy Gap," *Journal of Democracy* 13, no. 1 (January 2002): 99–112. On deliberalization, see Eberhard Kienle, *A Grand Delusion: Democracy and Economic Reform in Egypt* (London: I. B. Tauris, 2001). But see also Gwenn Okruhlik, "Networks of Dissent: Islam and Reform in Saudi Arabia," *Current History* 101, no. 651 (January 2002): 22–28; Diane Singerman, "The Politics of Emergency Rule in Egypt," *Current History* 101, no. 651 (January 2002): 29–35; Joshua A. Stacher, "Post-Islamist Rumblings in Egypt: The Emergence of the Wasat Party" (breakaways from the Muslim Brotherhood who wish to participate in the political system), *Middle East Journal* 56, no. 3 (Summer 2002): 415–32; and Larbi Sadiki, "The Search for Citizenship in Bin Ali's Tunisia," *Political Studies* 50, no. 3 (August 2002), 497–513. In Morocco's "first free and fair elections," in September 2002, Islamic "fundamentalists" tripled their seats (in an expanded 325-seat lower house) to become the third-largest party there: John Leicester, "Morocco Elections Hailed as New Era," *Boston Globe*, September 28, 2002; and "Elections in Morocco," http://www.election world.org/election/morocco.htm, October 10, 2002. Further east the next month, monarchial Bahrain's first parliamentary elections included women candidates: Somini Sengupta, "Bahrain Says 52% Vote Turnout Meets Democratic Goals," *New York Times*, October 25, 2002. Next door, Philip Taubman writes, even "Saudi Arabia Searches for a More Flexible Social Contract," *New York Times*, November 7, 2002. It is also worth remembering that electoral participation in Arab countries has a long pedigree: Ghada Hashem Talhami, "Syria: Islam, Arab Nationalism, and the Military," *Middle East Policy* 8, no. 4 (December 2001): 110–27, takes it back to the 1950s.

26. Henry and Springborg, *Globalization*, 160, 185, 193; but see also James B. Sauer, "Metaphysics and Economy: the Problem of Interest," *International Journal of Social Economics* 29, nos. 1–2 (2002): 97–118; and Masudul Alam Choudhury, "Microenterprise Development Using Islamic Financing and

Organization Instruments: Modality and Practicum," *International Journal of Social Economics* 29, nos. 1–2 (2002): 119–34. Choudhury, a Saudi also working in Canada, is one of the most prolific writers on Islamic financing, but there is a whole magazine put out by the Islamic Development Bank in Jeddah: *Islamic Economic Studies.*

27. These points are also registered in Henry and Springborg, *Globalization*, 115–16, and 211; and in Metcalf, "Islamic Activism," 5.

28. Neil MacFarquahar, "War and Politics: Gains by Islamists in Recent Elections Driven by Perceptions of a Hostile U.S.," *New York Times*, November 6, 2002. Pakistan and Turkey will provide important tests. The October 2002 elections gave Islamic parties a fifth of the seats in Pakistan's restored National Assembly: David Rohde, "Pakistani Fundamentalists and Other Opponents of Musharraf Do Well in Elections," *New York Times*, October 11, 2002. And within a month the latest version of Turkey's Islamist party, despite harassment, swept to an absolute majority and the right to lead the government again: Charles A. Radin, "Turkish Party of Islamic Roots Wins Election," *Boston Globe*, November 4, 2002; Ian Fisher, "Turkey Waits and Wonders: How Closely Bound to Islam Is Election Victor?" *New York Times*, November 7, 2002.

29. Metcalf, "Islamic Activism," 5–6.

30. On these thinkers, see John L. Esposito and John O. Voll, *Makers of Contemporary Islam* (Oxford: Oxford University Press, 2001). They and those who think like them are however highly vulnerable to backlash from political events: Thomas L. Friedman, "The Hidden Victims," *New York Times*, May 1, 2002. On regime adaptation and resilience, cf. Joseph Kostiner, *Middle Eastern Monarchies: The Challenge of Modernity* (Boulder, Colo.: Lynne Rienner, 2000).

31. A translation of the *fatwa* is in Ruthven, "Eleventh of September," 340.

32. On this dispersion and decentralization, cf. Vincent M. Cannistraro, "The War on Terror Enters Phase 2," *New York Times*, May 2, 2002; David Johnson, Don Van Natta, Jr., and Judith Miller, "Qaeda's New Links Increase Threats from Far-Flung Sites," *New York Times*, June 16, 2002; Douglas Frantz and Desmond Butler, "Fears of Isolated Copycat Attacks, Hard to Detect or Stop," *New York Times*, September 5, 2002; Don Van Natta, Jr., and David Johnston, "Signs of Revived Qaeda Are Seen in Latest Strikes and New Tapes," *New York Times*, October 13, 2002; and Douglas Frantz, "Al Qaeda Evolves into Looser Network, Experts Say," *New York Times*, October 15, 2002. But the Internet can lead away from as well as into Islamist extremism: Mahmoud Alinejad, "Coming to Terms with Modernity: Iranian Intellectuals and the Emerging Public Sphere," *Islam and Christian-Muslim Relations* 13, no. 1 (January 2002): 25–48; Mark Graham and Shahran Khosravi, "Reordering Public and Private in Iranian Cyberspace: Identity, Politics, and Mobilization," *Identities* 9, no. 2 (April–June 2002): 219–46; Pernilla Ouis, "Islamization as a Strategy of Reconciliation Between Modernity and Transition: Examples from Contemporary Arab Gulf States," *Identities* 13, no. 3 (July 2002): 315–34; and Nazila Fathi, "Iran's Students Step Up Reform Drive," *New York Times*, July 7, 2002. By November Iranian students were in the front lines of a major political crisis: cf. Nazila Fathi, "Protests Grow in Iran over Death Sentence for Professor," *New York Times*, November 13, 2002. Thomas L. Friedman generalizes from Iran to the Arab world in "Death to Dictators," *New York Times*, December 15, 2002. In fact, Friedman argues that the September 11 impact will be greatest not in the West, but in the "Arab-Muslim orbit": "After the Storm," *New York Times*, January 8, 2003.

33. For the post–September 11 period, John F. Burns, "Bin Laden Taunts U.S. and Praises Hijackers," *New York Times*, October 8, 2001; and the audiotape broadcast in November 2002, "Text: Bin Laden's Statement," *New York Times*, November 15, 2002. On the strategic landscape after Bin Laden resur-

faced, Peter L. Bergen, "Al Qaeda's New Tactics," *New York Times*, November 15, 2002.

34. Figures are from Larry C. Johnson, "The Declining Terrorist Threat," *New York Times*, July 10, 2001. Johnson is a former U.S. government counterterrorism coordinator.

35. It is hard to establish the trends concerning age and social profile for Islamist fighters with much confidence, probably because they vary from place to place and group to group. The Afghanistan-Pakistan-Kashmir fighters interviewed by Jessica Stern and Pankaj Mishra fit the Gamaa mold: Stern, "Pakistan's Jihad Culture," *Foreign Affairs* 79, no. 6 (November–December 2000): 115–26; and Pankaj Mishra, "Jihadis," *Granta* 77 (Spring 2002): 83–120. Yet the Central Asian organizations examined by Ahmed Rashid draw support from rural areas and farmers and from "amongst the urban intelligentsia: college students, educated but unemployed youth, factory workers, teachers" (Ahmed Rashid, *Jihad: The Rise of Militant Islam in Central Asia* [New Haven, Conn.: Yale University Press, 2002], 124, and *passim*). The link between higher education and Islamist radicalism has been recognized at least since Dale F. Eickelman drew scholarly attention to it in 1992 ("Mass Higher Education and the Religious Imagination in Contemporary Arab Societies," *American Ethnologist* 19, no. 4 [1992]: 643–55). Extensive interviews in Lebanon in the late 1990s supported the conclusion that respondents with higher status and education had much *less* enthusiasm for separating religion and politics than those below them on the social scale: Hilal Khashan and Lina Kreidie, "The Social and Economic Correlates of Islamic Religiosity," *World Affairs* 64, no. 2 (Fall 2001): 83–96. Awareness that "middle-class alienation rather than third-world deprivation" motivates many radicals is also penetrating large-circulation media: Nicholas D. Kristof, "Behind the Terrorists," *New York Times*, May 7, 2002; and Thomas L. Friedman, "Under the Arab Street," *New York Times*, October 23, 2002. The link is particularly strong in the Muslim diaspora in Europe and North America,

which furnished so many of the September 11 killers. Supranational and universalist radicalism comes naturally there: Chantal Saint-Blancat, "Islam in Diaspora: Between Reterritorialization and Extraterritoriality," *International Journal of Urban and Regional Research* 26, no. 1 (March 2002): 138–52. There are also fascinating crossovers, neotribalisms that almost bypass the city. According to London *Sunday Times* researchers, fifteen of the Saudi September 11 hijackers were from the mountainous province of Asir, formerly a semi-independent sultanate subdued by Faisal 'Abd al-Aziz in the 1920s and annexed in 1930; and a disproportionate number of their families can be traced back to Yemeni tribes defeated by (later) King al-Sa'ud: Ruthven, "The Eleventh of September," 351. Harking back to Hannah Arendt's *The Origins of Totalitarianism* on its fiftieth anniversary, Elisabeth Young-Bruehl in fact sees in Islamist terrorism the same triumphant supranationalism, basically antipolitical, that Arendt studied in Europe: "On the Origins of a New Totalitarianism," *Social Research* 69, no. 2 (Summer 2002): 567–78. So the "typical Islamist terrorist" is probably still the classic newly educated son of the first generation in the cities; see Elaine Sciolino, "Portrait of the Arab as a Young Radical," *New York Times*, September 22, 2002: "Born in Algeria, raised in France and reborn as an Islamic warrior."

36. David Rohde and C. J. Chivers, "Qaeda's Grocery Lists and Manuals of Killing," *New York Times*, March 17, 2002.

37. Ray Tayekh and Nikolas Gvosdev, "Do Terrorist Networks Need a Home?" *Washington Quarterly* 25, no. 3 (Summer 2002): 97–108. The answer is yes. "Al Qaeda's leaders, including Mr. bin Laden himself, are either dead, in prison, in hiding or on the run": James Risen and Dexter Filkins, "Qaeda Fighters Said to Return to Afghanistan," *New York Times*, September 10, 2002.

38. This was a point I made in "A War to End the Terrorist Era," *Boston Globe*, November 11, 2001. But others make it too, and in November 2002 the United States supplied punctuation

by killing a suspected al-Qaeda leader in Yemen with a missile fired from an unmanned drone plane: David Johnston and David Sanger, "Fatal Strike in Yemen Was Based on Rules Set Out by Bush," *New York Times*, November 6, 2002; and Robert Schlesinger, "Yemen Attack Expands Scope of War on Terrorism," *Boston Globe*, November 8, 2002.

39. For example, Noorhaidi Hasan, "Faith and Politics: The Rise of the Laskar Jihad in the Era of Transition in Indonesia," *Indonesia*, no. 73 (April 2002): 145–70; Jane Perlez, "With Indonesian Politics Up for Grabs, Islam's Role Grows," *New York Times*, April 30, 2002; and Raymond Bonner, "Southeast Asia Remains Fertile for Al Qaeda," *New York Times*, October 28, 2002. Much, however, pointed in other directions, for example, Indira A. R. Lakshmanan, "Radical Islam Finds Obstacles in Modern, Secular Indonesia," *Boston Globe*, October 20, 2002; Ralph Peters, "Turn East from Mecca: Islam's Future Will Be Decided on Its Frontiers," *Washington Post Outlook*, December 1, 2002; or C. J. Chivers, "Uzbek Militants' Decline Provides Clues to U.S.," *New York Times*, October 8, 2002. There are judicious surveys of the post–September 11 general landscape in Quentin Wiktorowicz, "The New Global Threat: Transnational Salafis and Jihad," *Middle East Policy* 8, no. 4 (December 2001): 18–39; and Martin Kramer, "Islamist Bubbles," *National Interest*, no. 68 (Summer 2002): 132–38: "a fervent remnant, however small, will soldier on" (137).

40. The U.S. government appeared to be acting accordingly, at least in some places, for example, James Dao, "U.S. Shifts Emphasis in Afghanistan to Security and Road Building," *New York Times*, November 12, 2002; and "Winning the Peace in Afghanistan," *New York Times*, November 21, 2002, an editorial applauding appropriation of an additional $3 billion over four years for reconstruction and expanded peacekeeping there.

Index